Demonology 101

K. W. Kesler

Copyright © 2011 Kurt Kesler

Smashwords edition

All rights reserved.

ISBN-13: **978-1301691906 (New Occult Reviews)**

*TO MY DAUGHTER AND WIFE,
WHO TAUGHT ME THE IMPORTANCE OF LOVE WILL OVERCOME
ANY DEMON, REGUARDLESS OF FAITH.*

CONTENTS

1	Demonology: An introduction	1
2	Demonical Possession	6
3	Conjuring and Banishment	14
4	The Historical Reference	21

The Guide

A: Pg. 31	N: Pg.120
B: Pg. 43	O: Pg.127
C: Pg.54	P: Pg.132
D: Pg.59	Q: Pg.142
E: Pg.64	R: Pg.148
F: Pg.67	S: Pg.162
G: Pg.73	T: Pg.191
H: Pg.78	U: Pg.200
I: Pg.83	V: Pg.206
J: Pg.88	W: Pg.219
K: Pg.92	X: Pg.223
L: Pg.100	Y: Pg.231
M: Pg.110	Z: Pg.238

Known Demonic Races	248
Bibliography and Suggested Reading	266

ACKNOWLEDGMENTS

To speak of another in this fashion I think is something that we all wish someone else would do for us all, I mean what really is an acknowledgment? It is a kind word to which a reader, who happens to have their name written in this section has a "warm and fuzzy" moment. I mean sure given light of the topic in which this book is written, most people who have to be acknowledged are actually dead. I am not trying to be a pessimist about the subject, however once you pass over, there is very little chance you sit around reading books in a nice quiet corner while there is another spirit in the opposite end of the room who looks at you with a menacing glare at you and you are wondering if he or she is evil and doesn't like you, or just wishes to do you harm. On that respect I would like to acknowledge every person, spirit or otherwise which has made contact with me in my life so far. I find that those who taught me albeit through expansion of my knowledge or by even those who treated me poorly even helped shape me, to the point of going on the travels I have had in my life, and the quest for the knowledge which I have gathered. So there it is, no names, no hints other than if you and I have crossed paths in my lifetime, then you are to be acknowledged. You have influenced this very project that you are reading. And to those who haven't had direct contact, don't fret! You to have shaped others, which in turn have shaped others, which in turn would cross a path eventually with those who I know, and now you have been acknowledged as well. So smile, in full smugness because you too are acknowledged.

Demonology:

An introduction

Ever since the beginning of recorded history there has been one word, Demon, the word itself may strike a form of fear into anyone. It has gained strength with fear over time. Most notably in the recent century when a man named Crowley spoke of them and later when a film called, The Exorcist hit cinema screens. But what per say is a demon? Is it nothing more than fantasy? Concocted by religious zealots? No, demons are better than that. They exist the very same way that we allow deities to exist. We created them. Through the universe there are energy sources and when we think about something we shape and form that energy into a form. We enable spirits and demons to exist. We charge the energy by thought and in turn the energy takes the shape of what it is we think about. We tell others about our concept of the being and then in turn others think and the energy gains power from it. So in the end, the demons, spirits and deities exist.

In order to successfully understand demonology, one must stop and unlearn the basic principles that one has learned from most religions. No true demon is beset to just one specific religion. Once a demon was thought about, and then created in one religion, the demon (much like gods and goddesses) were translated into other religions. Over time what started out as a certain type of demon just remains that type of demon, only there might be slight differences in appearance and habits. (Once again much like the gods and goddesses.) But above all else, the one thing that most in the modern age are mistaken about is that all demons are evil and or bad. Most people, because of the influence of religions such as Christianity, Jewish, and Muslim faiths, have gone into the thinking that all demons are evil, and their opposites, the Angels are good. This is false, as if read the basis of most theology beyond the big three faiths, you will begin to understand, that Angels much like demons can be evil as well. There are after all Arch-Angels, which have acted on their own and eventually outcaste out of Heaven. So yes the rule applies to demons as well, as history has been littered with the Arch-Demon, who in his or her own way upset the powers in charge of Hell and was eventually outcaste from there.

It is not the fault of those in the mainstream faiths; they were so strong in the belief that their "single deity" belief system, they in turn had to find room for all the leftovers from the plural deity system. And as for the "afterbirth" of the single deity belief system, aka Christianity, (before you close this book and call me a bad name, remember the Christian religion is built out of the belief of another belief system, so the term "afterbirth" is not meant with disrespect as it is meant as description.) it too has found its flaws in the belief system. Most Christians and even those who follow the Jewish-Muslim belief system fail to recognize that before Adam and Eve, it was Adam and Lilith. Yes that's right; Adam had a "marriage" before Eve was made. Now, why do most Christians fail to recognize this? Simple! The bible from its original form has been cut and pasted throughout the years. One of the worst offenders is the King James Version. When King James had his bible "correct" for his belief, almost 30% of the original text was removed. Also King James wasn't the only offender in the situation; others picked bits and pieces out of the bibles over the years. Ironically it was this very same restructuring that made Pope Gregory in the 6th century named Mary Magdalene a prostitute, which was later recounted by the Catholic Church in the 1969. Because it had been proven, (even though they of course follow the King James Version.) that there were almost forty pages in between Jesus meeting Mary the prostitute, and Mary Magdalene. And which brings us back to

Adam; he had a wife before Eve. Lilith was made at the very same moment as Adam. And because she was not made after, but during the creation of Adam, she felt as if she was "an equal" and when Adam told her to do something, she ignored it and eventually left Adam, where upon God took pity and formed Eve, who follow Adams wishes. Lilith was made into a demon, and later served "Satan" aka Lucifer when he was cast out of heaven later on. Much can be said about the anti-feminism the religion spoke of in its early beginnings. First in the Jewish bible, then later when the Muslims re-worked it into their Quran, and even when the Christians came along, if you were a woman, and didn't respect your male counterparts wishes, you were deemed nothing more than a demon, and eventually a witch by latter society (but that is another story.)

So the concepts of demons and angels has always existed, in one way shape and or form, through a multitude of religions, they were there and in some places, were eventually referred to as Gorgons or demigods by some faiths. This brings us to this basic question, who are the spirits we have created? They are nothing more than beings and or creatures that have re-invented themselves throughout the course of time. They were shaped by our constant shaping. The earliest forms of demons were the spirits that caused fear into most of the early tribal humans. They would hunt in packs, much like animals and then sea creatures in the forest or desert, and run in fear of them. Later as man began to develop the gods and their enemies, mankind would alter what we knew. And in some cases, the most extreme cases we have had humans possessed by a demon.

As for the religious influences, please be aware, it does not really matter which faith you follow. Due to the fact that most religions that rely on the single deity (and to any formal Christians who believe in the trinity, remember by your definition, the father, son and holy ghost, it is supposed to still be the same being) and cannot consider the concept of plural deities and are opposed to it, Christianity in particular is subject of shattering. It is the one religion that has not only over 20 different forms currently in worship on the planet but has actually over 100 variations that were phased out over the centuries (yes even a church that believed Mary Magdalene was Jesus' wife. Also four more churches at least are around that believed Jesus was a polygamist and had four wives, which would seem conceivable due to the fact most men were polygamist in biblical times.)

Demoniacal Possession

A demonic possession is a human (or in some cases animals.) Who has become inhabited or "taken over" by a demon and who is subject to the demon possessing the possessed. It is mentioned in the New Testament, in Mark, Chapter 5, and verse 12. Josephus also mentions a method of exorcism prescribed by Solomon, which had "prevailed or succeeded greatly among them down to the present time." Unfortunately, Josephus does not describe the method used to perform the exorcism. The current ritual is based upon other rituals that have passed from one religion to another and eventually made its way to Christianity. This is actually sad, because Christianity, Judaism and the Muslim faiths have shown itself to be one of the weakest religions to ward of a demonic possession. The priest, rabbi, preacher or prophet who conducts exorcisms usually goes into the situation with fear. In other religions however there is a better chance of not drawing out the ritual for days on end, as the demon is subjected to being compromised to an earlier stage in its existence. Demons hate witchcraft. Witchcraft unlike the holy prayers conducted by one of the "big three" religions have it as a rule to be able to call upon the spirits and vanquish them.

Only the big three religions actually give the spirit the ability to take over a human at will, and hold on to them to torment those around them. So yes, the real big news to you all is simple, if you, or someone you know is possessed then do not call a preacher, priest or rabbi. Find the nearest knowledgeable witch. You will find out the situation will clear itself up quicker and with much more lasting effects. Let alone as proven with some Catholic procedures, there won't be a need to bury the dead afterwards (they do have a reputation for that.)

Now, there is a well deserved thought that what in early history to be called "demon possession" would today in fact, be referred to as mental illness, and treated with the required care only a good psychiatrist and medications would offer. However, there have been a few cases of possession do seem to crop up from time to time, and the Roman Catholic Church does continue to perform exorcisms for those in need and if the subject in question has proven itself to not be a case of mental illness. Through the course of history, there have been many thoughts by historians that there have been increases and decreases in demonic activity. These are mostly based in the big three religions, however even atheist whom do not believe in religions have admitted that there might be cases in history in which the "dark forces" did spring up and wreak havoc. Most cases in history can be filed away with the concept that humans are humans and commit acts against other humans. However some have shown that according to dates presented in prophecies that the increase of demonic possession has collapsed economies and caused famine. Some older historians claim that there is a rise in demonic activity during the destruction of Jerusalem, or during the Fall of Rome. Others have pointed out the French revolution and have linked the rise in Nazism during the early part of the 20th century. I will admit that yes Hitler's obsession with the occult does lend some light to the Nazi theory, and of course the use of the symbolism in the Nazi regime at the time doesn't help. There was even a theory of human/demon hybrids roaming the planet. The most notable one of these was Rasputin. A man who was, shot multiple times, stabbed, and beaten in the very same day, He only finally came to death after he was drawn, quartered and burned into ashes.

Which lends to the concept that demonic hybrid grants the person abilities such as Rasputin and others have exhibited in history. Some people who were possessed actually predicted the future and showed other psychic powers as well. The early religious followers had faith in the words spoken by those who were believed to be under demonic possession. They referred to these people sometimes as oracles or prophets. It should be duly noted however that modern psychologist and even professors of psychologist have been involved with cases of schizophrenia make specific and surprising prophecies which all resulted in perfectly accurate predictions of events that eventually took place. In most cases science has been baffled and cannot make statements to explain these events. However, there are some who are willing to lend thought to the concept that there is a link between altered mental states and psychic ability. I myself have experienced such events as I fasted for a few days and found an euphoric state of mind that lasted for weeks after. Some are willing to proceed to the concept of the use of Ouija Boards, however only those trained in the use of witchcraft actually have the required knowledge to carry out such procedures. And without the knowledge one should have with Ouiji Boards, one can end up leading to a misuse of the device and as seen in the film The Exorcist, be lead into possession.

Now, some people have had experiences in their life in which they have been attacked by a demon. Allow me to set up the situation, you are asleep then you wake up with what can only be described as the full weight of a full being on top of your stomach, chest or back and you can't move a muscle. I mean seriously, you cannot move anything, not even your tongue. See I know about this, because I too have experienced this. In most cases as others have stated, they have seen things. Most notably an old woman (the "old-hag" syndrome), and in some cases a full blown demonic apparition. Most chalk this up to oneself being still within the dream state and their sub-conscious mind is merely "filling in the blanks". I being a strong supporter of common sense and science love this way of thinking. It's a rational explanation to what has happened. But, in my case and some others it doesn't make the situation explained. I saw a reflection.

I was living in the campus district of the Ohio State University. The particular house I had been living in for the past year had given me all sorts of odd feelings. I normally was a "basement-dweller" the better part of my "campus life." I loved it, and then because of an off rush of odd events, my friends had decided to view a house on the northern end, and rent it. They knew it had a basement, and figured I would live there. I didn't care, because I like my other three roomies all worked nights mostly (in fact it was because of this, they agreed to the lease without really seeing the place. It was described as a four bedroom house, and knowing I would sleep in the basement, we just considered the fourth bedroom to be our "computer room."We showed up and were ready to move in. I walked to the basement and felt very uneasy. 2 of my three roommates all walked into what was supposed to be my new room and stood there in shock. There was a well in the room. And the room wasn't a room. It was the supports for the house, and there were two walls with brick, and the other two walls were nothing other than dirt. Needless to say, when I said, "I'm not sleeping down here." There was no one saying, "at least try it." We all had that creepy feeling down there. So, I made my room upstairs, and we just agreed we could keep the computer room in the main room, just those were into a "gaming frenzy" would keep it down for those trying to watch the main TV in the house, which is funny because we all still had TVs in our own rooms, and two of us also had a second computer in our room (yes, we are nerds and geeks because this was 2001.)

So I lay in my bed, on my stomach and that is when it happened, I woke up, paralyzed. I kept hearing something moving behind me, I tried to talk or at least make a noise, but my vocal chords had gone numb. I was an avid paranormal researcher the better part of my life, I knew what this was, and because I had learned to dismiss things like this as my mind just trying to make up for the fact, that I woke up out of sleep so fast, my muscles had yet to unlock themselves, hence the sleep paralysis. And as for the noises at the foot of my bed, they were just my mind, "filling in the gaps". But then something happened, that made me change my thinking. A pencil, I hear it tapping itself on the floor as whatever it was moving around. Then I heard the pencil roll, and to make matters worse, I heard it and then saw it roll on the floor, right past my TV, so I happen to let my eyes drift up to the TV. And then in the reflection of myself, and the room reflected back at me in the glass of the TV screen, I saw it. I was amazed, and then almost on the point of laughter. Like I said, I knew better then to trust this, after all my mind had just been filling in the blanks right? But then I stopped that 3 seconds of wanting to laugh at the concept my mind was hallucinating, because another pencil rolled across the floor, and that's when it had struck me, I was not hallucinating the demonic black figure moving around at the foot of my bed and making noise as I lay paralyzed on my stomach in bed. I began to muster all the chance of breath I could. I found endlessly over a hundred times a second to move a muscle so I could leave. Nothing I did would allow me to move. And then I heard the noise, that allowed fear to get the better part of me, I heard what sounded like a small grunt from the foot of my bed. And I immediately passed out. When I awoke, I saw both the pencils were where they had rolled too.

I had a few more experiences in that house that were on the same level. In a few cases, a roommate's girlfriend would get scared over something along these lines, and another roommate would "hallucinate" his dead brother, who transformed into a demon-like creature before he too passed out. I guess the hardest part was the fact that after we left, we found out that other people who had lived there had horrid experiences as well. But the worst was 3 years after we had moved out; I was living in a nearby suburb and had heard there was a recent suicide in the house. But it didn't end there, because a year after that, the house burnt down, and the found the remains of what can only be described as a "devil / demon worshipping cult" artifacts, from the early 1920s in the basements dirt walls, buried just 5 feet in. Now I will admit I can recognize the difference between a devil worshipper and modern day Satanist.

Satanist are for the better degree, atheist. But during the time of Crowley, it was not uncommon to find those who used more powerful magick then those of today's covens.

So with that, I learned that there was a world in-between religion and science. A world, between common sense, and mysticism, there was a world in which demons and angels do exist, and so do all the Gods and in most cases it isn't if we are willing to let them in as it is if we are willing to let them play.

Conjuring and Banishing

The concept of conjuring a spirit is not something new or even by definition is not "Satanic" or even Witchcraft for that matter. Conjuring has taken place throughout history, though most associate it with Witchcraft and Satanism, however it is in fact much older of concept and in its use, even Christians conjure spirits. The earliest Christians, also known as the Catholics, would invoke spirits such as saints and of course that of the God Jehovah and or the spirit of Jesus Christ. In most of the early Jewish periods, Jehovah and even the prophet Moses was invoked, as invoking a spirit is nothing more than a fancy word for conjuring, which is why most consider the practice to be Witchcraft by basis. By conjuring can take practice and more importantly knowledge.

Knowing how to conjure a spirit is the equally as important as knowing how to banish. With most Christian conjuring it is recommended that one would fast for at least a few days (if not the idea of forty days) as this would prepare one for the enlightening experience, and show that one is true to the words they will speak. I, myself have noticed that just a few days will work, however regardless of how long you fast, you should at least take some multi-vitamins during the process as you are a human being and it is a well known fact that prolonged intake of substance can lead to death, which the only invoking or conjuring you will be a part of will be the spirit being called for. Keeping in mind with the use of conjuring make sure that you know what the likes and dislikes of the spirit you are summoning as they will show for what they like and can be banished from your environment by their dislikes. If you are a Christian calling for a demon, the moral implications are between you and your faith, however by calling an Egyptian demon, remember that regardless of how much faith you have in your own religion, it is not as effective against them and others not bound by Jehovah or his son. The use of Jehovah might work some however as of course the slaves of Egypt were Jewish. And it is known that some of the Kabbalah Demonic spirits are prone to being dismissed through the use of Jehovah, however invoking Jesus Christ for banishment of those demons generally does NOT work. You may get some peace and quiet, but you will no doubt be back to square one in a short period. The main reason why "men of the cloth" or Priest or Preachers have more success is because they usually are trained on the matters, hence before you conjure a spirit and in turn banish a spirit, it is best to expand your knowledge.

The first basic reason why in most Christian based exorcisms have some success is because of the use of Holy Water. Now Holy Water is of course not so much a new invention, Witches, Shaman and even the modern Wiccans use a version of "Holy Water" as it is nothing more than water, salt and positive energy reinforcing. Now Christians much like each group would like to claim their water is the strongest (Yes I have heard an argument between a Christian and a Wiccan that each ones water was stronger, ironically in the Wiccan's "Moonbeam Water" actually got rid of the demon.) as for who is the strongest there is a simple way to ensure whatever your faith is, your water will work wonders, make sure the salt level is a good amount. Most Demonic or negative energies cannot handle salt. Sure casting or banishing with salt alone is a great idea on paper, but there is something about salt once it is dissolved into water that makes the impact, after some experimenting I have found it has in some part to do with the fact that water is a great conductor of energy. However it should be noted, the salt with its nature for cleansing, and water with its energy conducting capabilities are merely a salt water solution without positive "blessings" Regardless of which faith you follow, each one has a positive part (yes, even Satanism has a positive side, though they might not own up to it.) and it is this positive blessings that the water becomes fully energized. So when banishing a demon, which of course is nothing more than a combined effort of negative energy(ies) then it becomes the obvious in banishment to use a "Holy Water". If you are unsure what the proper blessings to perform for the water, please consult your faiths literature and or clergy in how to achieve this.

The use of Talismans in calling forth a spirit or in this case demon is something that should not be taken lightly. You must of course have the proper talisman to call forth the specific spirit that you are trying to conjure. It is very much like the coins that certain Christians use in calling to a specific angel. However in this case the talismans are commonly made from wrought iron, bronze, pewter or even silver. I recommend pewter as this has shown the best results. They are generally between 2 inches to 5 inches in diameter, and will have the symbol that is commonly used or associated with that spirit. The following is some examples. It should be noted that a proper talisman should have a copy of the symbol or "seal" on one side and the other side should be left blank. In some cases the talismans that have been produced have had a "conjure spell" on the reverse of the coin; however this causes the talisman to "go into overload". The seal coin (also sometimes called religious metals) are nothing more than the "calling card" of the spirit in question, it should not be considered the "phone that which the calling cards number is used", by placing a conjure spell or spirit conjuring on the reverse of the seal, you in effect are overloading it by being on "constant redial", hence the spirit in question will realize this, and much like a lot of humans who receive constant bothering from being called, will begin to ignore the phone, so if you wish for your talisman to be correct, then do your calling without the instructions on the coin to do so.

The seals listed in the guide are the known seals of the known demons which range primarily from the Solomon Era. They were generally out of the Kabbalah sources for higher magick and should not be reproduced in Talisman form unless you are serious about conjuring one, there are many demons who still use their Solomon seals for calling upon them, and there are ones who have in effect changed their seals or "changed their number to a private listing" only the trusted Shaman who work with these spirits know the newer symbols. If you are being harassed by a demon, it is not uncommon for the demons seal to appear to you in an unheard of place, as either the demon has placed it there or a person who wishes the spirit to harass you has placed it there.

The Guide:

How to understand and use the guide

The following guide is presented in alphabetical order. It is broken down further beyond the demon name with the known origins of its existence. When you see it is mentioned in "Christian Demonology", it should be noted that it is not from direct Christian origins however. It came from the original Jewish influences and then translated into the Christian mythos. If you see that it is considered "Kabbalah Demonology" it should be noted that it comes from that specific Jewish mythos, which is more witchcraft than religion. If you see "Mixed demonology" it means that is one of the known demons that made its presence known in multiple religions virtually all at once. I tracked down the origins of others when possible, such as Slavic and certain Asian text, but if no known religion was linked to a specific demon, I felt it best to leave it blank.

This listing will show the known individual listings for specific known demons and the lore surrounding them. When a description is known about them, it too is put in to act as a "field guide" After the alphabetical order is established; I included a listing of known types of demons. Certain demons might not be known by name, however their Clan and or demon race is known, you will find it in this section. As for the use as some have stated that there are demonic spirits that have disguised themselves within literature or fiction writing, I chose it best to leave them out. I myself have studied the Lovecraft mythos, and do find striking similarities between the Cthulhu Fhtagn (Ka-Thu-lu Fa-Tha-Ghan) Mythos and some of the early Kabbalah, Christian and especially Sumerian mythos, even some Aztekian basics as well. However, until we can separate successfully demonic fact from fiction, I think it is best concentrate on the powers of normal demonic forms. I will admit the recent events of the Cthulu sightings in 1967, and the sightings in Highgate Cemetery in 1969 are excellent reports, and the subsequence sounds of Cthulu opening R'lyeh in 1997 in the Pacific Ocean during the one true time of capturing the Cult of Cthulu in the middle of the "Ceremony of Ghradiashka" does actually steer oneself into warranting them in the list, the talismans are now long lost, and until there is a proper way to call upon them, they appear to have no influence upon mankind. So, with that established, please enjoy the knowledge presented and happy hunting and or conjuring!

The Historical Reference: How to know where the religions and histories of the demon.

Knowing the origins of a Demon or spirit is almost as important as knowing the name of one. In some cases a demon on the listing might be listed as "Mixed" this is due to the fact the demon in question actually is a combination of two different spirits that have "collided" at some point in history, the previous spirits no longer exist, and the new version has attributes of the previous two. The following is a small guide to help you understand the subjects a bit better.

- **African / Tribal:** These demons, though some like to consider them a part of Egyptian history are far from it. These demons originated from the tribes and counter tribes that formed in the time period of 2,300 BC through 500 AD. The easiest way to attract them is through water and food, preferably animal. However don't just run off to a market and get that steak just yet. Much like all basics in all religions, the food must be a sacrifice of some sort. I can recommend that if you are not a hunter you can purchase animals which are sold alive for food, such as mice, rats or even rabbits. In your offering you should field dress the creature, for those of you unaware this would entail removing the inner body organs. It is a common practice in all earlier religions, including Judaism and even early Christianity (Though most Christians do not either know, or in some cases wish to even believe there is enough historic records showing that their religion too participated in sacrificial offerings.) The easiest way to remove the demon is by making "Moonbeam Water" and sprinkling it over and throughout your dwelling. Also salt in general is a good measure. These demons are born of the desert; salt is the one physical thing they will automatically respond too.

- **Asian / Chinese / Japanese:** Most Americans hear the word Asian and they assume Chinese or Japanese, however in the scheme of things, Asian does not limit itself to the two concepts. Asian demons are from anywhere albeit it the aforementioned subjects or even India, or anywhere in fact on the Asian pantheons. There are some Asian demons that dwell or hail from the countries of Australia, or even New Zealand. It is best to have more knowledge on the specific demon that you are in contact with before proceeding. It should be noted that though the demon may be have more of a historic reference to Chinese or Japanese cultures, there is still the underlying Asian philosophies, to which it is best to follow the concepts brought forth from those philosophies when calling upon and or banishing.

- **Aztecan:** Now these demons are interesting in that they actually from the Mayan religion, they were just known to become inert for some years and time periods, until man reappeared in the region long enough to allow those sparks of energy to cause the demons to reemerge into the next religion, which is not an uncommon practice as with one religion or concept of thought gets passed along through to another culture, and even in some cases another language, let alone race is how religions for the better degree have been doing things on this planet for at least the past 6,000+ years, (and longer as some religions that have managed to have been discovered are far, far older) The Aztecan / Mayan Demons are amazing in that some have even adapted into Christian based beliefs, however it is known that there is of course the running out of the Mayan calendar in 2012, which is ironic as on December 20th (one day before the end) the Demons in question are said to been given one day of freedom on the planet.... I can only guess we will see how well this goes. The biggest thing is to bear in mind that the Aztecan aspect has caused the Mayan Demons to be controlled to some Christian abilities; however the Mayan roots do grow strong in the fold, which is why it is best to have a woman dominate and control them for banishment.

- **Christian:** When a demon has its origins from Christian mythology, there is an essence that that the demon in question is against Christ or his father Jehovah. In most cases this is true however it should be pointed out to the reader that that is not the case in every situation, basic Christian folklore and mythology generally apply, however remember these demons do not like Christ, so yes a cross will no doubt disturb your time with the demon if you are trying to conjure it.

- **Druidic/ Celtic:** These demons are known from the Celtic race. They were the barbarians of the early times before the standard structure religions that managed to become the main source of energy for human's thoughts. The Celtic barbarians were known to invade the areas where the Druids were, and even though some have suggested that the Celts "left the peaceful Druids alone", the truth is, and no they didn't. And we do know this because the DNA mapping back to the era of 3,000 BC shows that there were influxes of Celtic blood, generally through Male to Female (Hence, you guessed it, they came, saw Druidic Women and raped them) Where upon the DNA mapping does show a loss for Celtic Males (So yes they killed the men and raped the women. Not the "peace-loving romantics" of modern myth.) The best ways to fight or banish a demon from this concept is through the use of moonstone, hematite, frankincense and wormwood. Crush the frankincense and wormwood to a powder, and store it in a glass jar for no less than one fortnight (2 weeks) and then place the powder mixture in an item for burning such as an ashtray, and ignite the powder which should burn very similar to incense. If you are trying to attract one of these demons, I must warn you that the demons are very violent much like the Celtic and eventually Druids who bore them, as a Celtic pastime was to throw a child into a pit with no less than 4 hungry dogs and watch what happens. The demons from this background are known for their same love affair with torment and violence.

- **Egyptian:** Though there are some similarities with these races of demonic spirits, it should be known that one of the best ways to combat them would be in the use of Kabbalah Magick. You have to remember the Kabbalah is magick that some scholars have shown that the Kabbalah gave birth to the Jewish religion, though there are those who believe the religion came about and the Kabbalah just happened to be the pagan/witchcraft based religion that was influenced by the

Torah. In either case, Kabbalah Magick or Witchcraft seems to have some of the strongest effects on Egyptian demons.

- **Hindu:** These Demons are some of the most powerful demons that have ever formed from the power of human shaping. They are known for their cruelty and even worse their intent on causing a human to suffer to the point of death no less. The one thing that helps is eating a common Hindu dish called, Vindaloo. There is a mixture of spices, combined with Vinegary potatoes and tomatoes that cause the demons to not be attracted to the human once the human begins to secrete the oils through the skin. Most Westerners fail this and actually have become the most harassed by the Hindu Demons as most Westerners are not fond of eating Hindu dishes. As I have experienced on the matter, I tell people to just begin to eating, and Christians have actually enjoyed the effects of eating a dish called "Tikka Masala" as this dish will actually attract angelic spirits to you. But the attraction of Angels is another subject and another book entirely.

- **Kabbalah:** A demon whose origins are that of the Kabbalah, are usually obtained through higher magick use then that of the average wiccan, Kabbalah is based off of Hebrew Magick and in most cases, the Torah will work against them, however remember that the raiser of these are of course Witches, not WICCANS. Wiccans rarely entangle themselves in the use of conjuring a spirit, Witches for the better degree do, and most Kabbalah conjuring spells are known to be some of the strongest. Most Christian mythology will work against them as the christen mythos is bound by Jehovah in the end.

- **Muslim:** These demons for the better degree are some of the very weakest amongst demons, when the holy war began between Allah and Jehovah, the Muslim based demons actually fought for Satan against Allah, and being Satan, he used the Muslim based demons as pawns. Though some are strong, most have a severe weakness, and it is known that in some cases, some Muslim demons have actually been destroyed by a human child.

- **Native American:** These dark spirits are the product much similar to the Mayan, however for the better degree, they have remained in purer form compared the Aztecan influence of Christianity. The best way to banish you and your property of these spirits is to lay down crushed lime. If you can lay a trail of lime surrounding your property no less than 1 inch thick, and stay inside for at least 4 hours (so yes a night's sleep will work), Native American Demons become easily distracted and cannot see or sense clearly what is happening on the other side of the lime, so they will leave and go elsewhere. Even in the highest cases of a demonic attraction from a Native American demon to a human has this happened? They lose interest. You can also spread the lime over your lawn to cause a "mist" they will not cross as well.

- **Nordic:** The Nordic demons have shown their great love of fish, beer and wood. If you wish to banish I would suggest a strong word of advice, you can't. Though Nordic demons are much at a power loss against positive energies, they do NOT give up. Once the demon leaves, the demon will remember and when you least suspect it shows back up. In some cases the person who called for the spirit has suffered the wrath of the spirit because once you summon them, they will always need a new challenge, if you are unable to provide a new challenge for the spirit, then they have a tendency to keep bugging you. Yes there is a blessing, because once the spirit is done with its task, and if it happens to be summoned by another it will leave you alone on its own accord, but once that task is done, the demon will spend the rest of your life and the other person who summoned its' life re-appearing and waiting for another task.

- **Slavic:** The Slavic histories have secured a good position for demonologist, as this is where some of the most powerful demons that are still currently in power are from. The concept of mountains filled with minerals and ores gave more energy during the formation of the spirits, and that combined with some of the earliest Christian fighting which of course with war and death comes a great energy release, has caused the Slavic based demons some of the very strongest. The typical anti-negativity items are what you need to use to banish silver, garlic and of course salt.

- **Sumerian:** 5,000 years before Christ, the Sumerian religion was the main form on earth, and in the main pantheons their gods ruled. After Jehovah made his launch for rule of the main pantheon in the heavens, the darker spirits took their place in the new rulings as demonic beings. They are known for their love of cheese, almonds, honey and spices such as cinnamon. If you are calling for one it is generally best to use one if not all of those to attract them, however to banish you must use any wine that has sat uncorked for a fortnight, as the newer vinegar is known to be harsh for them, they also of course do not like salt, but I strongly suggest you use sea salt for banishment as the modern table salt will work, but you may have to use more.

A

Abaddon: (Kabbalah Demonology) King of the Demons of Hell (Revelations 9:11) He is also known as Apollyon in the Greek mythos. His name is from the Hebrew root meaning "to destroy" The biggest thing about him, is that he has a "cocky" attitude and even though he and Satan are supposed to be on the same side, he does not follow Satan's' orders. He has been known to act as neutral as possible, because ultimately he is out for himself. And he often is said to have the ability to advise humans by posing as another human.

Abdiel: (Christian Demonology) From the Arabic word "Abd" meaning slave. He is said to have the influence of man to cause them to enslave another man through either direct slavery or low wages.

Abigor: (Christian demonology) Commanding 60 legions, he is described that he rides a horse and carries a scepter and lance. He is known for his cruelty upon the homeless and indigent.

Abraxas: (Egyptian Demonology) The Basilidian sect of the Gnostics of the second century claimed Abraxas as their supreme god, and said that Jesus Christ was only a phantom sent to earth by him. They believed that his name contained great mysteries, as it was composed of the seven Greek letters which form the number 365. They constantly refer to him as; "Abraxas, to whom they attributed 365 virtues, one for each day." The older mythologists placed him among the number of Egyptian gods, and demonologists have described him as a demon, with the head of a rooster, a huge belly, a knotted tail and serpents instead of legs. He is represented on ancient amulets, with a whip in his hand. It is from his name that the mystic word, Abracadabra, is taken.

Adramelech: (Christian Demonology) Where he is chancellor and president of The High Council of Devils, he took his job during the Sumerian phase of history and has remained there ever since. He is considered an Arch Demon whose name means, "King of Fire". He has a love of tormenting children by causing them to be burned.

Agares: (Muslim Demonology) First Duke of the East in the Muslim mythology and commands 31 legions in Christian mythology. He is known to appear willingly to those who call upon a "spirit" during a spirit calling, and he is known to have a fondness for getting humans to commit suicide. *(see seal symbol on opposite page)*

Agathion: (Christian Demonology) Also called Agathodemon, by the Egyptians which is where the world gets the name demon from. He was worshipped by the demons, though once the Jewish and Christians faiths began their misinterpretations of religions, Agathion began to take the evil form he is said to love to torment those of faith. A demon which was said to appear only at midday. However it is said he can stay around until sundown. It took the shape of a man or a beast, or even enclosed itself in a talisman, bottle, or magic ring.

Agramon: (Christian Demonology) Demon of fear, he thrives his power on causing those to be in fear. It is said the best haunted house attractions must pay homage to Agramon.

Agratbatmahlaht: (Christian Demonology) One of Satan's wives, and demoness of prostitutes. She is known as a succubus who causes her to only be reflective in a mirror as an "old hag", however she may retain her looks of beauty until it is said a man has an orgasm because of her, whereupon the man sees what he would in a mirrors reflection.

Alocer: (Christian demonology) A Grand Duke of Hell who commands thirty-six legions of devils. He is described with lion's face, and is usually appeared dressed as a knight with a teal green armor and on a Black horse. He supposedly causes animals to attack humans, which he takes joy in.

Aitvaras: (Slavic Gypsy Conjuring) A little demon, that appears in the shape of a black cat, or a black rooster. He will give goods and money to those who sell their souls to him; things he stole from other people. Aitvaras usually nests behind the stove, and the inhabitants often leave food and drink for him.

Amduscius: (Christian Demonology) A Great Duke in Hell who commands 29 legions of devils. He rarely takes human form and is prone to look like a unicorn. He is the reason why the parent groups started panicking during the great "Satanic Panic" of the 1970s and 1980s, because he is prone to encourage youth to "live in fantasy."

Amane: (Kabbalah Demonology) According to the Book of Enoch, he was the leader of the two hundred angels who rebelled against God, and swore allegiance to Lucifer. Once Lucifer was caught, Amane went into hiding on earth and is considered neutral because he found the god Jehovah to be cruel and not worthy of his love.

Amazel: (Christian Demonology) Chief of the goat-demons or "hairy demons", he runs the goat demonic army for Satan and is as ruthless to his own troops as he is in tormenting human-kind.

Amduscias: (Christian Demonology) This demon of disturbing music continually plays the internal rhymes and riddles internally to reinstate the programming if it is ever touched. This demon then is responsible for the programs to continue running. This demon, whose internal music acts as an alter system he is considered to be the Grand Duke of Hades Commander of twenty-nine legions. When evoked, appears in human shape. He gives concerts, at the command of men, where one hears the sound of all kinds of instruments but can see nothing. It is said that the trees themselves bend to his voice. And he is a producer of disturbing music.

Andras: (Christian demonology) Marquis of Hell who commands thirty legions of devils. In Egyptian Mythos, this demon was a female, and is described in both mythos as having a bird head with angel-like wings. She is rumored to have a likeness, for the taste of rodents such as mice. He is very well known for his love of making humans commit ritualistic murders.

DEMONOLOGY 101

Angul: (Asian Demonology) Pronounced Ann-Gull, not Angel, she is a demon from the Asian folklore that kills other women with an axe if they do not offer their men to her as servants.

Akop: (Mixed Demonology) A demon from the Hawaiian folklore that preys on widowed people. This demon is known for going to the "Mainland" and even around the planet, however very prone to remaining in the Hawaiian Island Chain.

Apepi:(Egyptian Demonology) A serpent demon that in ancient Egypt was in opposition to the sun god Ra, and also known as Apophis under the Greek and Roman Mythos. He is known as Asmodeus a demon of wrath, In the Christian myth; he was the angel who was banished by Raphael, according to the Book of Tobit 8:3

Asag:(Sumerian Demonology) He is known to be the demon that causes sickness A terrible demon from Sumerian legend responsible for draught and plague. He is described as a large, round, three-legged, three-armed creature with no neck and several eyes covering their entire bulk. Has dark, hardened skin that feels like rock when touched, and is considered by many to be almost indestructible.

Asmoday:(Christian Demonology) Prince of demons, thought to be the serpent that deceived Eve. He has been confused with Satan and his role from time to time. *(See seal symbol on next page)*

Seal of Asmoday

Astaroth: (Christian Demonology) In Hell he is The Lord Treasurer and the Grand Duke of Western Hell. He is Duke over 40 legions. He is known for his likeness of tempting humans with their greed. Was once a female and a goddess of lust, before he tempted an Rabbi. *(See seal symbol on next page)*

Seal of Astaroth

Astarte: (Celtic Demonology) A Celtic heathen god, who is sometimes consigned to Hell due to his Barbarian ways, she is known to be the creator of the Celtic pastime to throw small children into a pit of hungry dogs for entertainment. When the Christians came to power, Satan took her as a bride and proclaimed her "Queen of spirits". And made all those who entered hell have to be kissed by her in order to receive some form of mercy from him.

Atamas: (Christian Demonology) Said to inhabit nightmares and known for his cruelty to those who seek revenge.

Aym: (Christian Demonology) He is a Great Duke, who commands 26 legions. In heaven, Aym was the guardian of the eastern edge. Lucifer managed to gain Ayms trust by getting God (Jehovah) to admit Aym's creation was a mistake because of his skin color, in Angelic form was blue. In demonic form, he still retains his blue color and is known as the demon that temps those who have suffered with sexual molestation.

Ayperos: (Christian Demonology) A Prince of Hell who commands thirty-six legions of devils. He has a love of drunken debauchery when humans consume alcohol and either commits adultery or sex out of wed-lock.

Azazel: (Christian Demonology) Also known as Satanel, he is the Standard Bearer of the armies of Hell. He is Satan's direct bloodline to the throne of Hell.

Azika: (Muslim demonology) The God of Witchcraft, he is known as an outcast to the Muslim god Allah because Azika believed women should have godlike powers and was banished by Allah. Has three heads which is stated that a witch would call upon him and gaze into each set of his eyes would grow their magickal powers.

Azrael: (Muslim demonology) He is known as angel of death. Though started in the Muslim Myth, he has transversed into the other faiths. The legend says that if someone makes him smile, then a disaster of either man made or natural takes place and there is loads of death. It is said that the demonic face shown in the smoke during 9-11 was the face of Azreal.

B

Bael: (Christian Demonology) Commanding General, of the Infernal Armies of 66 legions. He is known to resemble the concept of the appearance most think of the devil. Red in color, with horns. He is depicted as a creature with three heads - a cat, a crowned man and a toad. His pudgy torso ends in a spider's legs. Those who invoke him are made alert and cunning and are taught the means of making themselves invisible when necessary. He is a demon cited in the Grand Grimoire and head of the infernal powers.

Baalberith: (Kabbalah Demonology) Also known as Berith, he is the Chief Secretary of Hell. He is known to be Satan's male lover. He is depicted as a pontiff seated among princes of the infernal regions. Originally he was the Phoenician (Canaanite) god of covenants. He was one of the demons who possessed an Ursuline nun at Aix-en-Provence in 1610.

Balam: (Christian Demonology) Terrible king with three hearts, but no soul, he commands 40 legions. He wears a royal crown, surmounting two long and upward horns, and a pair of extremely hairy ears sticks out at right angles from his skull. The sharp, goat-like facial features are enhanced by a long, scraggly beard. His limbs terminate in unnaturally long fingers and toes, capped by sharp-pointed nails that look as deadly as the claws of the goshawk perching on his right wrist. Balam, once an angel of the Order of Dominations, is quite easily invoked and relatively harmless to deal with. Like many of his species, he answers questions concerning past, present and future events, and he is willing to reveal the secret of invisibility. He is an excellent teacher of the subtle art of cunning, and he imparts wit and finesse to whoever queries him on these matters.

Balan: (Kabbalah Demonology) A Prince of Hell, he is one of Satan's sons. He has a fondness for killing sea life, and wreaking havoc for sailors. He often disguises himself as a Mer-man, and uses Mer-maids as a form of bait, for people sailing above the waves. *(See seal symbol on next page)*

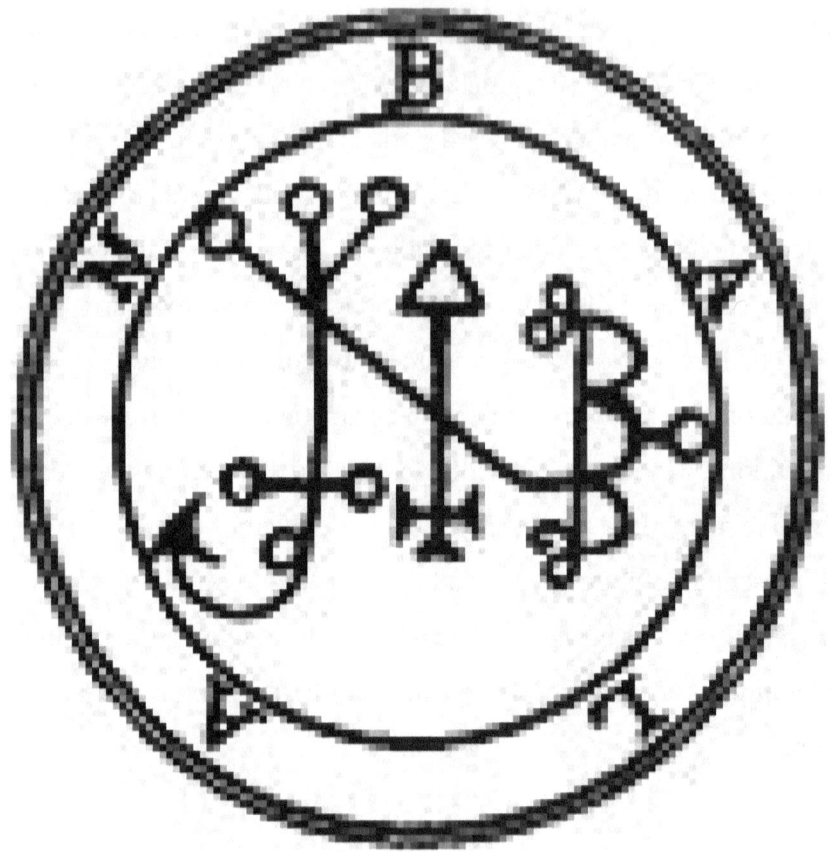

Seal of Balan

Baltazo: (Christian Demonology) The Demon who possessed Nicole Aubry of Laon in 1566, he went to dine with her husband under the pretext of freeing her from demon possession, which he did not accomplish. It was observed that at supper he did not drink, which showed that certain demons are averse to water. It should be noted that this very demon was recently reported in 2011 possessing a woman in Texas, and that the use of water was very effective.

Baphomet: (Kabbalah Demonology) God of the Templars, and Worshiped as Satan by the Early Romans. The Templar's are thought, by some, to be one of the earliest sects of Demonolatry. When Christianity took hold, he was given a high spot on Satan's council of 12.

Bar-Lgura; (Kabbalah demonology) A gargoyle type demon, which is said to sit atop houses and then pounce on the inhabitants, he has a fondness for hearing dogs bark and howl.

Bast: (Egyptian Demonology) The goddess of witchcraft and sexual magick in the Egyptian pantheon, if you ever had the urge to do anything of a bizarre sexual nature, you were entering the realm of Bast. Often identified as the Egyptian cat goddess, Bast is one of the most ancient forms of Babylon, the Mother goddess. Bast is portrayed as both a cat and lion. As the goddess of sexual magick, she ruled over lust and sexual heat. Bast is readily identified as the Beast because she "presided" over the vast sexual experiments of Atlantis (and later Egypt) which gave rise to mermaids, minotaurs, centaurs, Pegasus and the like. Bast's legacy gives us at least two words in our modem lexicon. The word "bastard" was derived from the Pandora's Box that opened with the unrestricted breeding practices that were common during her reign. During the reign of the goddess, paternity was not an issue. Marriage came into being in large part due to the need to preserve a patriarchal structure for inheritance and succession purposes. When the Jehovah took over, he made parentage an issue and punished women who bore children outside of the established tradition of wedlock. This is not so much a moral issue as a power issue. Crowley's concept of the Scarlet Woman or Babalon is another name for the goddess Bast. Scarlet is chosen because it is the color of blood (also the color chosen for the cover of The Book of the Law). As stated earlier, blood represents the passage of the moon and the menstrual period. The lunar calendar is therefore the calendar of Bast and represents the true time line. This is in direct opposition to the Gregorian calendar that was given to us by the decree of Pope Gregory, the same pope who authorized the inquisition. In regard to her lunar aspect, Bast's offspring were known as children of the moon, hence the name moon child.

Bearded: (Unknown) (Mixed Demonology.) This demon, his real name is not revealed so that people do not deal with him when searching for the Philosopher's Stone. He is said to dwell below ground and would be the one responsible for any attack upon a human and their blood was drained.

Beelzebub: (Sumerian Demonology) Name means the 'lord of the flies', a high demon of hell that is sometimes equated with Satan. However it is not Satan himself.

Belial: (Christian Demonology) Also known as Beliel and Beliar. The Prince of Trickery, the Demon of Sodomy, and the Antichrist, he is said to cause humans to behave with "about wickedness and guilt"

Belphegor: (Mixed demonology) The demon of Ingenious Discoveries and Wealth, he commands fifty legions of devils in Hell and is said to show a soft spot for infants.

Berith: (Christian Demonology) Great Duke of hell, who governs 26 legions, appears as a red soldier on a red horse. He is known by the Egyptians as a good demon. In human form he takes on the role of a female. According to the detailed description of the seventy-two major demons, Spirits of Solomon as put forth in the Lemegeton, he can only be safely summoned with the help of magic rings, bearing his specific seal. Berith's voice is clear and persuasive, but he is a notorious liar. Anything he says must be weighed with great care, though he does reveal the past and the future. Berith also has the power to transmute all base metals into gold; thus he is sometimes known as the demon helper to the unscrupulous alchemists. In books on magical recipes, Berith is associated with a method of conjuring him under a form resembling a mandragora. On a Monday night a black chicken is bled at a crossroads. One must say: 'Berith will do all my work for twenty years and I shall recompense him.' Or else one may write the spell on a piece of virgin parchment with the chicken's blood. The demon thus evoked will appear the same day, and put himself completely at the conjuror's disposal. But after twenty years, Berith will claim his reward for services rendered. *(See seal symbol on next page)*

Seal of Berith

Bonifarce: (Christian Demonology) One of the two demons said to have been successfully exorcised from Elisabeth Allier in 1639 by Francois Faconnet. The two demons who had possessed her for twenty years admitted that they had entered her body by means of a crust of bread they had put into her mouth when she was seven years old. They fled from her body in the presence of the Holy Sacrament. The name of the other demon was Bonifarce Orgeuil.

Botis: (Christian Demonology) Appears as a viper, and proclaims the past and future. He is the demon of gift with the right sacrifice. He is even so bold as to deny a deity passage to the past or future from the present. It is even stated that the "all-known" god Jehovah must use his services in order to gain access to past or future time. His dwelling is said to be in the deserts of Utah, not far from Salt Lake City.

Buer: (Christian Demonology) President of hell, of the second order, and commanding 50 legions, he is known as the deceiver of those who unite faith. He likes to tempt those who will be unto Jehovah, and has even been known to tempt those who follow Satan with a promise of heaven. He is one of the most powerful demons as he once drank the blood of Jehovah, Lucifer (during the 2nd holy war in the ever-realm) and eventually the blood of Jesus Christ. (He posed as a follower, and helped wrap the corpse.)

C

Caym: (Christian Demonology) The Grand President of Hell, which has been known to take the form of a large thrush (bird). He may be the grand president, but he only rules 30 legions. He has been known to have a softer side in that he was willing to extend "the olive branch" between Hell and Heaven during the crisis when the humans revolted against the Gods before Jehovah took over from Zeus. He is supposed to inspire knowledge of the liberal arts and to incite homicide. This fiend is said to be able to render people invisible.

Charon: (Mixed Demonology) The boatman of Hell who takes souls across the Styx. When Jehovah/Allah came to power, he was given a son, Azreal. Before humans were created, Charon himself was considered to be the god of light, Later when Hades needed someone to guard the underworld, the task went to Charon. Eventually when Jehovah came to reign, Charon was considered be freed of his time.

He is said to roam the forest and punish those who do not respect nature.

Chax: (Christian Demonology) A Grand Duke of Hell who is also fond of tormenting those who try to cheat at gambling. He will stop at nothing to find the one who cheats and then torment them to the point of death no less. It is known that a lot of Casinos will hire Shamen and Conjurers to call upon his spirit to protect the Casino.

Chernobog: (Mixed demonology) Also known as Yin in Chinese culture. He is a Slavic demon whose name means "The Black God". He brings all things evil at night. He is the guardian of Mount Athos (Not Bald Mountain). He is known to shine kindly on the gypsies in the area, especially those who follow the ruling of magick.

Chemosit: (African Demonology) A demon from Kenya who is half man and half bird. Said to be the very demon who talked tribal leaders into selling out their own people for slavery.

Chu Kwai: (Chinese Demonology) Also known as Sen Chun, she is a demon from China, the creator of freaks.

Congo Zandor : (Mixed Demonology) A Demon worshipped in Haiti. He/She (appears in both forms.) is prone to liking strong alcohol, and sea water. Though worshipped, has been known to have a mean streak if its subjects are mistreated.

Creb-Fad: (Muslim Demonology) A very head strong Assasin Demon that took over for Creb-Xa upon his death. Has a massive hatred of Allah and is said to be the one who cause the prophet Muhammad's Death.

Creb-Moc: (Muslim Demonology) This demon is well known to guide those for who are willing to sacrifice themselves against Allah. He is aided by his Wife, Creb-Rahak

Creb-Rahak: (Muslim Demonology) She follows her husband and his goal of destroying Allah with the help of humans who they teach.

Creb-Xa: (Muslim Demonology) Head Assassin. Demon, Worked briefly for Zeus, then Jehovah during the 1st Holy War. Switched sides, when Jehovah created Allah and then Allah began to have Creb-Xa gather up small children for Allah's bed chamber. Creb-Xa felt it was beneath him to act as "pimp".

Cresil: (Christian Demonology) She is another of Satan's wives. The demon of laziness and impurity. She has been known to possess humans with recorded record since at least 1811. Some who have performed exorcisms with this specific demon, they believe that she is the demonic form of Elizabeth Bathory.

Crocell: (Christian Demonology) Grand Duke who appears as an angel, and governs 48 legions. Legend has it he had a thing for eating the brains of dead angels during the 2nd, 3rd, and 4th "Holy Wars". He is described as always shown in yellow with a single horn in his head. Some theorize his death has taken place as he was not present in the past 3 wars between the underworld and heavens.

Cyrmon: (Christian Demonology) Arch Fallen Angel, one of the original 1,000 who fought with Lucifer to get rid of Jehovah. He is considered to be a "neutral-good demon" as since he is upset with Lucifer; he acts for his own will. Is said to take on a human female mate every 200 years. He had a talent for being a "Personnel Manager" and is believed to have gotten himself in leagues with men such as presidents of countries in order to felicitate his own wishes albeit good or evil.

D

Dagon: (Mixed Demonology) The Baker of Hell, formerly a serpent god. She supposedly was the witch in the folklore tale of Hansel and Gretel. She is known as the typical embodiment of a witch when people dress as witches for All Hallows Eve. She has been known to encamp herself in places where she can remain and allow her prey to enter. She has the mastery of "kitchen witchery" and is known to be able to take items such as human fat and make it into a pie. In other words, yes she does eat humans, but not directly.

Dahaka: (Christian Demonology) Was once a An ancient Persian god of death and demon of deceit and mendacity. He loves destroying life. Dahaka is usually depicted with three heads, while scorpions and lizards crawl all over his body. Now it is said he takes on other forms and lives within the North American Northwest. Has a fondness for tormenting remaining Native tribes and the loggers in the area.

Deumos: (Christian Demonology) Another of Satan's wives, she is a female demon was once married to Jehovah and shared her bed with Allah. She was cast out by Allah when refused to bear him a child. Supposedly has a talent for causing men to become Jealous.

Deumas: (Sumerian Demonology) He has a crown, four horns on his head, and four crooked teeth in his enormous mouth. He has a sharp, crooked nose, feet like a rooster, and holds in his claws a soul he is about to devour.

Dev: (Muslim Demonology) Also known as Decarabia, in Persian mythology, he is described as a demon of enormous power, a ruthless and immoral god of war. Once Jehovah ruled Allah out of the Main Pantheon and the Internal Holy Wars began, Dev made a pact with Allah to thwart Jehovah and his Son from power. However Allah being Allah, Dev was banished and swore revenge against Allah.

The seal of Dev, aka Decarabia

Devil: (See Lucifer)

Donar: (Celtic Demonology) German god of thunder, forerunner of Thor. His symbol is the swastika. Oak trees are sacred to Donar. During the Second World War, he is said to have wiped out a Nazi platoon group, because they mauled their way through a forest and destroyed many Oak trees. The only survivor came back and described the demon was on a large scale. With a head the size of a tank, and the body of a mansion, he is described as purple and green with thousands of eyes and tentacles. Once the solder had came back to tell the tale, he was taken to the spot in France where it had happened. He was shot on the spot as the corpses of the dead are described as looking "digested whole." And the officers believed the soldier to be insane.

Dian: (Christian Demonology.) In Irish mythology, the Tuatha are descendants of the great mother-goddess Dana. With her consort Bilé, Dana engendered a race of gods who have their counterparts in the Celtic mythologies of Great Britain and Gaul. The gods of early Irish mythology reappear as a legendary account of the history of Ireland since the great flood described in the Bible. The Tuatha retreat to the Tir na n-Og, a distant land of eternal youth, and live on in subterranean palaces, where they maintain an invisible, fairy presence in Ireland.

Demoriel: (Christian Demonology.) A demon, which is said to live and posses those who live in the southern part of the United States, he is prone to picking on those where the decedents of slave owners who mistreated their slaves. No one knows where the demon originated, however there are those who have claimed to have interacted with the demon that he is from West African mythology.

E

Eblis: (Christian Demonology) He is the second brother of Satan. The legend has it, when Jehovah came to power; he took on the goddess Athena as his 5th wife. (Remember even in all religions, the gods and humans were polygamist.) When the making of Angels came around, Eblis or Entrotus as he was called, followed his brother Lucifer into the fight against the gods, and he too was cast out. His name means 'despair'.

Elathan: (Christian Demonology) A Celtic lord of Darkness, whom eventually was deemed a demon by the Christian Church, he is known for his love of tormenting those who fear the dark and the unknown.

Egyn: (Mixed Demonology) A demon that is as powerful as Satan, especially when the death of a child takes place. He has been found setting traps for children. Some stated that he gains more power when the child shows signs of sloth. And in 2004 was found to be the possessing factor in a fast food chains playground in California. (No names of business, but they have a clown.) It is reported that he possessed 4 children in one week and one death took place, after the child began speaking in tongues and vomiting then fled his parents into traffic.

Erebus: (Christian Demonology) A demon which guards the darkness around Hell, He is married to his sister, Nyx. Together they are a constant thorn in the side of married couples. Though they are married themselves they both work in their own way to split couples up before they have had a chance to combine and make offspring.

Eurynomus: (Mixed Demonology) A Prince of Hell who likes to feed on the dead. He has escaped and shown himself in human demonic possession. He is fond of possessing a human during the winter months.

F

Fash: (Mixed Demonology) This arch-demon is considered a neutral demon as he has a hatred of Satan for destroying his human family he took in the early dark ages. Supposedly Satan killed his family but not before raping the women and causing those to spawn off his children. He is very powerful in the fact he understands the full effect of cause and effect. He knows what will happen if you take a step and pause for 1 second instead of immediately taking another step and how just that one second pauses could forever shape and form your destiny.

Fene: (Slavic Demonology) As the opposite of Isten, the god of light, Fene is also the name of the place where demons roam. The Demon itself has a succubus effect on both men and women. She is known for her capable hands at running brothels, both human and demonic.

Flauras: (Christian Demonology) This demon along with the demon Andras are attached to alters who must commit ritual murders. He appears in the shape of a terrible leopard. When he assumes a human shape, he has a frightful face and blood-red eyes. He knows the past, present and future, but unless commanded into the triangle he will deceive the exorcist. He incites demons or spirits against his enemies, the exorcists, and he commands twenty legions. He converses gladly of divinity and the creation of the world, as also of the fall of spirits, his own included.

Focalor: (Mixed Demonology) A demon that drowns men and overthrows ships of war, he has a love for the sea, and loves to twist up a sea battle. He is described as taking on human form, with darkened blood red eyes, and a human type skin, though noted as having this pale blue tone to it (Almost as if the corpse was dead for a few days.) The last known time he was seen and reported was the 27th of May, 1941. As for the German sailors who survived the sinking of the Battleship Bismarck claimed a person in officer uniform threw what looked like a "bundled amount" of dynamite into the ammunitions loading hatch for main gun #2. They claimed this was done after the announcement that the ship was alright for the sailing back to France for repairs. They same German sailors also claimed that after the explosion had taken place from the dynamite, they saw the officer laughing and saying "watch this!" At which the explosion that blew main gun out of hits cradle and the ship began sinking. This information was finally shown to the public during the 1970s.

Foras: (Christian Demonology) Grand President and Knight of Hell, commander of twenty-nine legions. He knows the properties of herbs and precious stones. He teaches logic, esthetics, chiromancy, pyromancy and rhetoric. He can make a man invisible, inventive and adept in the use of words. This demon is knowledgeable. It can teach logic, the virtues of herbs, how to live long and supposedly how to become invisible. It can appear as a strong man in human form. He can locate lost objects and is depicted as a rotting corpse of an old man.

Forau: (Kabbalah Demonology) One of the demons who serves Hades, he is a brigadier general of the infernal legions. He has knowledge of skilled military knowhow. Some have compared him in the holy wars as a demonic version of George S. Patton. Some theorize that it was because of his tactics in the 8th Holy War which cause the delay of Jesus by a 1,000 years due to the damage that had to be restored and fixed.

Fujin:(Japanese Demonology) The Japanese god of the wind and one of the eldest Shinto gods. He was present at the creation of the world and when he first let the winds out of his bag, they cleared the morning mists and filled the space between heaven and earth so the sun shone. He is portrayed as a terrifying dark demon wearing a leopard skin, carrying a large bag of winds on his shoulders.

Furfur:(Mixed Demonology) A Count of Hell who commands twenty six legions of demons. He is said to have been a Muslim solider during the crusades, and eventually was cursed by a Slavic Witch. He was took the appearance of a wolf, until a large outbreak of panic over werewolves in Wallachia took place, and he was killed. When he entered Hell, Satan himself was pleased with his acceptance of the satanic ways. So much that Satan rewarded him with a royal order of Count Hood. There was a report that in the 1930s when Satan was on earth, he found a human woman who bore him a daughter and that daughter is married to Furfur.

DEMONOLOGY 101

G

Gaap: (Kabbalah Demonology) A great president and prince, appears when the sun is in the southern signs, coming in a human shape, and proceeded by four powerful kings. He loves to make men insensible, gives instruction in the consecration of things which belong to the divination of Amaymon, his king, delivers familiars out of the custody of Sorcerers, and gives true answers as to past, present and future, transports men speedily from place to place at the will of the exorcist. According to Weyer, he will speak outside the triangle, but what he says will be false. He is known as a rapist and is prone to do it to women, both god and or human.

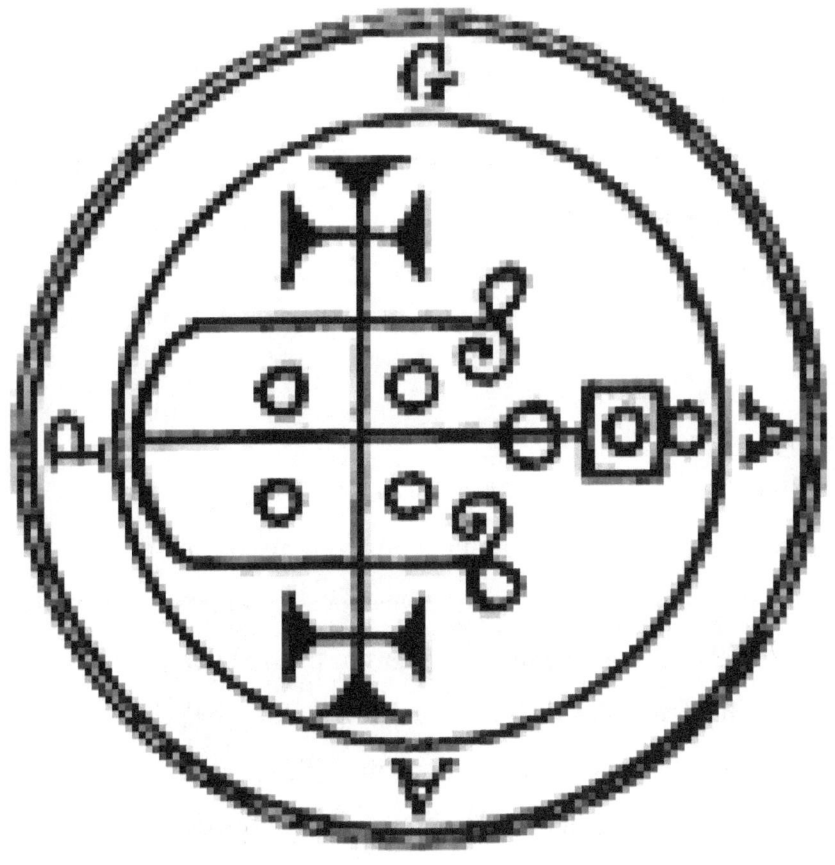

Gamygyn: (Slavic Demonology) A great marquis, appearing in the form of a small horse or ass, but afterwards in human shape. He speaks hoarsely, giving news of souls who have died in sin. He summons into the presence of the exorcist the souls of drowned men, and of those detained in Purgatory, called magickally Cartagra - that is, the affliction of souls. They assume an aerial body, are visible to sight, and reply to questions.

Garm: (Nordic Demonology) Is the hound which stands in front of Hell's Home and snarls with jaws dripping blood at pilgrims from the upper world.

Geb-Shal: (Christian Demonology) Assassin Demon, she loves to combine torture into her assignations. According to Christian Mythos, she was once the lover of Jesus once he returned from earth. However, Jesus found out she was a part of the 4th attempt to overthrow his father Jehovah and was sent to earth for punishment. (She was spared Hell due to her courtship with Jesus, and Jehovah knew Satan would use her as a vessel to create more demi-gods.) She is said to inhabit Europe until the recent 1990s where visions of her have been found for hire in the American North East.

Ghaddar: (Slavic Demonology) A female demon in the deserts of the Red Sea countries, It catches travelers and tortures them by devouring their genitals. She has been recently seen by Lake Superior as of 2010.

Glowbx: (Kabbalah Demonology) Demon with a strong hate of man, he has been found in Georgia and Northern Florida as it is prone to sleeping in the red Clay, and tormenting those who speak to Jesus on a daily basis. He loves to cause a "Miracle" then reverse it once the caller feels like they have finally gotten the hope they asked for.

Goap: (Christian Demonology) Prince of the western region of Hell, he spent time in purgatory due to the fact he even tried to over throw Satan. Jehovah allowed him to remain at his seat in order to cause disruption in the "un-holy" lands. It is rumored that Allah gave him sanction on earth for a period due to the fact he enabled Muhammad to have his 6 year old bride, Aisha. When Aisha's mother protested, Goap sealed her mouth shut.

Guseyn: (Mixed Demonology) Arch-Demon, under the command of Jehovah, he was the one who tormented the Rabbis after they had the Pontius Pilate order Jesus to death. He is said to have slain their families and drive them all mad over the course of a few years. He is said to find home in Germany, in the forest near the River Rhine.

Guta: (Slavic Demonology) A greatly feared demon that beats his victims to death with the limbs of their offspring and or loved ones, he has been said to always smell like raw sewage and appears in the form of man with six arms.

H

Haborym: (Christian Demonology) This is a demon of fire who is placed in control of the fire around the internal hell pit. He is the first son of Satan. A Duke of Hell, commander of twenty-six legions. He is the demon of fire and holocausts. Depicted as a three-headed monster, a cat, a man and a snake he is usually sitting astride a viper and brandishing a torch. He is willing to perform whatever tasks his father asks.

Hatu-Atu-Topun: (Asian Demonology) Also known as Hetu-Ahin, she is a female demon from whom stalks twilight and dawn. She is reported to have had a few human possessions and loves to torment those who are engaged in sexual activity during the twilight and dawn hours. She has a strong hatred of other woman, because she is considered a jilted lover in Asian myths.

Haures: (Kabbalah Demonology) Strong Duke of hell and commands 20 legions and is very frightful as he is a Cyclops, towering just over the average man with one sole horn atop his head. We know he still occasionally comes to Earth and torments people, and as recently as 2009

Hecate: (Mixed Demonology) In Greek mythology, she was the goddess of sorcery and witchcraft and was especially worshiped by magicians and witches, who sacrificed black lambs and black dogs to her. She is known to be in the United States along the western seaboard. She has a fondness for possessing young children, because it torments the adults.

Hedammu: (Kabbalah Demonology) A Hurrian snake-like demon which lives in the sea, He has been known to lay waste to ships and has attacked humans in the Mediterranean. He is described as 60 feet long with a row of horns down his spine and white in color. There were reports as recent as 2009 of his sightings. It is said that he does have a human form, which is used to lure prey to his location, whereupon he switches back to his normal self and attacks.

Herensugue: (Muslim Demonology) An evil serpent, from the early crusades in the 11th century, all is known is Allah provided this to protect his people when Jehovah proceeded to deny Allah's claim to power after the treaty signed amongst the gods after the very last holy war in the alternative dimensions which surround ours and earth was to be the "last battlefield." Allah is said to have given the demon the power to store the bodies of who it devours, never digesting them and vomit them back up to throw off the enemy. This might explain the bodies of what appeared to be early "Christian crusaders "dressed from the 12th century that were found in Iraq in 2004. And the subsequent reports of a large "sandworm."

Homod: (Egyptian Demonology) A demon, who hails as RA's head assassin, he has actually been sighted in the cities that host Egyptian artifacts from the Tutankhamen, on display in museums. He is described as a "centaur" type creature, as his torso is human and his lower half is the back part of scarab. He is known to attack the homeless and vagrants near the museums which are displaying the exhibits. Very few survive, and those who do speak up just to be treated as a mental health patient.

Hutjin: (Christian Demonology) The demon ambassador to Heaven. He is known to be wonderful at playing chess (and even beat Jehovah) and of course negotiates with the high councils concerning the "grey area" souls. He has a love for coming to Earth and tempting young females into changing their lifestyles into one that pleases him.

Hyskel:(Mixed Demonology) He is from an alternative dimension; he has the pleasure of killing protectors. It is said that whenever a police officer is killed, Hyskel is smiling. He will aid anyone, especially those who murder or harm the innocent. He has a strong distaste for authority and order, and is well known to have become a formal lover of the Goddess Eris and will come to her if she calls.

I

Iak-Sakkak: (Kabbalah Demonology) A demon, who watches over the gates of Hell. He is compared to the opposite Saint Peter in respects that he doesn't watch over the wrong people getting into hell as he makes sure spirits that aren't permitted don't leave.

Ibego: (Slavic Demonology) He is a demon of destruction. He is described as a demon that takes both human form and can enlarge himself into a larger form in the shape of what looks like a large dark blue praying mantis. His human form however is noted he appears normal except he is noted to have a greenish hue to his skin and a blue hue to his hair, with small horns / bones that pierce through his skin at his basic joints. (It is described as small bone-like horns piercing through his knuckles and so forth.) He is spotted throughout most of Europe, with most notable whenever there are accidents or massacres. Ironically it is noted that he was spotted in 1908 near Lake Baikal and was seen after the Tunguska "event" and later was reported by Chernobyl before and after the disaster there. Whenever there are mass suicides and killings throughout Europe and Asia, there have been reports of him. (It should be noted that the Chernobyl incident it was reported by a person seeing him change from human to his demonic form and back again. Which, is either because he was active in creating a situation or as some demonologist theorize, mass radiation causes demons to not control their shape shifting capabilities that well.

Ibwa:(Asian Demonology) she is described as a demon, who feeds on dead bodies and known to cause chaos so she can eat. Likes to appear as a teenage girl and seduce men. Whom she lures into confidence and then murders them and eats their flesh.

Ikwaokinyapippilele:(Aztecan Demonology) A strangely named demon from who causes illness, and suffering. He has been spotted in recent years in the Brazilian jungle. Has the shape of a giant ant with eight snakes for arms, and wnigs like a bat. And all this plus it is said to be twenty feet tall.

Inmai: (Christian Demonology) A demon from Myanmar who bizarrely lives in the post in front of houses and causes people to be inured with thorns.

Ipos: (Christian Demonology) Demon count of Hell, who commands 36 legions. He is reported to looks like a lion-headed angel, and has been known to possess humans on occasion. Most recently as of 2007 in Hull, UK and in 2009 in Toledo, Ohio. *(See seal symbol on next page)*

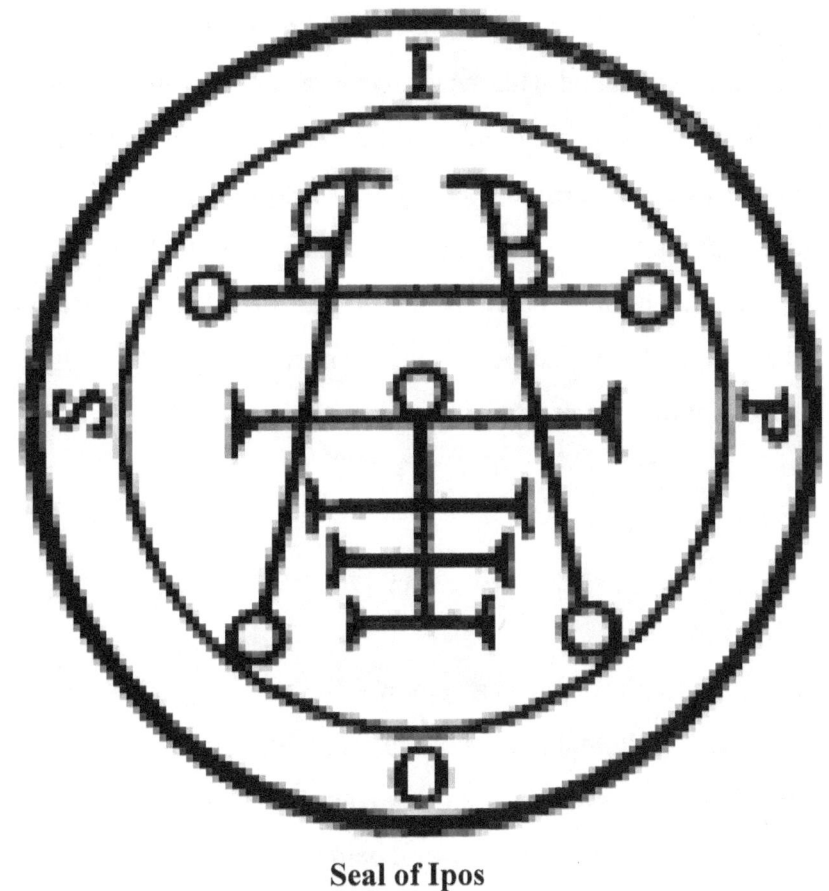

Seal of Ipos

Irvene: (Christian Demonology) Demon dog that lives on the Canary Islands, he has a knack for causing people to commit suicide from drowning if they don't feed him.

Ishtar :

(Mixed Demonology) Chief goddess of the Babylonians and the Assyrians and the counterpart of Astarte, a Phoenician goddess. Under modern Christian rights, she seduced Jehovah when he was taking over from Zeus, and was his lover until the uprising from Lucifer. She was found with the sacred scrolls that would unlock Jehovah's power hood from his celestial being and was in a brief alliance with Lucifer. But the story doesn't stop there. She offered to hand the scrolls of these magickal incantations over to Allah (Lucifer wasn't worried because Allah's deity power is not full.) and Jehovah cast her into hell. She escapes on occasion from Hell and possesses humans (Not making bad movies with her name.)

Itzcoliuhqui:

(Mixed Demonology) She is a demon goddess whom is prone to be a succubus to human males and both females. She is about empowering women fully. Allah, Jehovah and even Odin have all had their run ins with her (The worst being Allah, when she used her powers to hold Christ in a paralyzed state, and then had Allah kiss the behind of Christ in front of the spirit of the prophet Muhammad upon his death and entrance into the "heavens", which she did as reported to crush the whole spirit of recently dead prophet.) If you are a man, it is best you do not trust her, and best left to have a female friend discuss something with her. She perceives men, the way men have perceived women throughout time, so in her eyes you will not get a fare wage, forced to do housework and so on.

J

Jahi: (Mixed Demonology) She is a female arch-demon., who specializes in debauchery. She is rumored to have been a concubine of Allah before he came to power of his realm, and was used by him to seduce his enemies. Once she had completed her tasks, he banished her from the heavens and was sent to Earth. It is rumored she has been in the adult entertainment industry and is quite capable of taking a solid human form long enough to work. Though don't look for her in mainstream pornography. She is prone to the extreme.

Jezebeth: (Kabbalah Demonology) She is the demon of falsehoods. She speaks to whoever lends her an ear. She is known to possess humans and animals; most recently as of 2010 a case was reported of a farmer who listens to her through a horse. In which he killed 51 of his cows, and when Jezebeth took possession of his wife, he took his own life.

Jilaiya: (Indian Demonology) Flies as the bird of the night and sucks blood of the names it has heard, It can only suck the blood from people whose name it has heard.

Jin Laut: (Mixed Demonology) Once a part of the Jinn clan of demons he is also an Indonesian sea demon. In Japanese mythology, he is a servant of the goddess of the southern ocean, who can kill a person by sitting on his chest, and knocking the air out of a person's lungs. Though in modern time he appears to have an almost incubus ability, and equal to delivering an "old hag" message to humans who cross his path.

Joja: (Christian Demonology) Demon from unknown origins, most have seen the demon form when they come into contact. Reptilian skin, glowing blue eyes and a taste for human feces. Some people consider this demon to be more or less neutral.

Jormungandr: (Mixed Demonology) Is the great dragon which lives in the Ocean-Stream which runs around Midgard (Nordic), during the bringing of the mono-deity system of beliefs, he was resurrected as a demon, which can take a human form and transform into dragon form demon. He was cast into demon-hood due to his strong mindset from his previous incarnation. He liked to eat virgin women, and after the onset of Jehovah, he was told to stop, but he elected to not do it. He eventually was capture by the Angels Michael, Raguel and Hayyel. Brought before Jehovah, he merely stated he "enjoyed doing it". Upon hearing that Jehovah cast into purgatory. He was later released by Chinese dragon worshippers in the late 9th century. Where upon it is said, "He crossed over through the gate, and wiped out the entire virgin population of the village."

Junier:(Christian Demonology) Prince of the demonic angels, He is one of the few who transverse the Heaven to Gateway daily. When souls are standing upon the gateways into these realms, and are rejected, he is the "prison guard." He is known to have the ability to cast someone into and out of purgatory with his gaze, and has even sent deities into purgatory with his power (Even Jehovah during the 2nd Holy War for "safe keeping."

K

Kabrakan:(Mixed Demonology) A giant demon in the Mayan mythos, which can cause earthquakes. His power makes mountains disappear, while his power can also make mountains rise, also through earthquakes. In Greek, he was referred to as a Titan, and his name was the Kraken.

Kaitabha:(Hindu Demonology) The Hindu demon which tried to attack Brahma. However, Brahma spotted them, and invoked the goddess Mahamaya. At this point, Vishnu awoke, and the demon was vanquished into purgatory.

Kalb: (Egyptian Demonology) A demon known for her intolerance towards children, she loves to pull the "old hag" routine on them, and though most chalk what happened to them as a child, alone in their rooms as their mind getting the better part of them with the "monsters in the closet". It is said it was most likely her. She thrives on fear, and can cause muse-like imagination in children.

Kali: (Mixed Demonology) She began with a Hindu base to existence and has since grown throughout the known pantheons. Born as the Goddess daughter of Shiva, the destroyer, she later would work for Allah in his attempts to gain full control. She would later be cast out of the heavens and sent to earth. Though some say she is more of an arch-demon as she no longer is willing to take any side other than herself, she is a known succubus who likes to attack her prey after an event.

Karau: (Aztecan Demonology) A demon from Panama who causes death in the world. Guards animals and protects them from the world, brings death to thoughts that would harm an animal.

Kasdeya: (Kabbalah Demonology) Known as the 'Fifth Satan'. From the "Book of Enoch", she is the fifth child of Satan. However some theorize that she would be the direct one to ascend his throne, due to the fact Satan known's this would infuriate the gods Allah, and Jehovah beyond comprehension. (Bear in mind, Even under Christian Reign, let alone Muslim, The gods; Jehovah and Allah are still prone to a "woman walks behind a man" way of thinking. So with that said the theory of her ascension to Satan's throne does ring some merit.) The theory has been under serious thought for the past millennium as she has not made her presence known outside of those who have reported from the realm of Hell, other than that she is under constant guard in Satan's Palace in Northern Hell.

Khanzab: (Muslim Demonology) A demon that disturbs the prayers of Muslims, thus causing doubt in their minds, he has been spotted in New York near the "Ground Zero" site of 9-11. According to sources, he was hired by an extreme Christian fundamentalist group to tempt those Muslims who visited the site, albeit because they are there to gloat or to mourn into Christian service. Normally I would pass this off as propaganda, however there have been a higher amount of Muslims converting into Christianity (and even Judaism, witchcraft and other religions.) after they visit the site to pay their respects. In human form he is said to have the appearance of a well mannered, good looking human Middle Eastern male. In Demonic form he is described as having a purple skin color, and four eyes, one forward, one left, one right, and one behind. He is also said to not have a mouth as his "mouth" is in the middle of his chest.

Keron-Kenken:(Christian Demonology) He is known as the demon which takes the life of infants. He eats the newborn's soul and drinks the tears of the mothers when she sleeps. He is described in the typical "gargoyle" appearance, and is said to be found at recent locations when an infant has died of SIDS.

Kigatilik:(Native American Demonology), A fanged demon and the enemy of priests, Described with the wings of an eagle, and the body of a horse, with the head of a fanged human.

Kingu: (Kabbalah Demonology) Also known as Kimaris, The demon in Mesopotamian myth who became the second consort of the goddess Tiamat, after her first consort Apsu had been slain. She gave him the Tablets of Destiny and intended to make him lord of the gods. He was sent to purgatory and eventually freed by Druidic witches, who were eventually slaughtered by their actions.

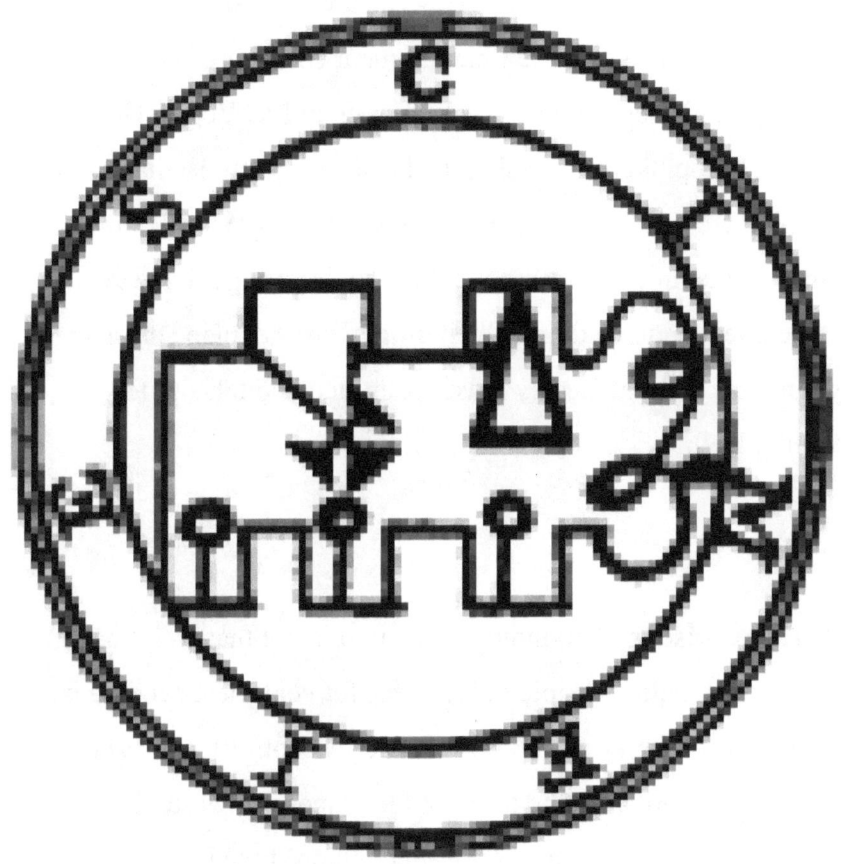

Klotilde: (Kabbalah Demonology) This spirit demands that the slave never get involved in human love. To love with human love would be to suffer. He is very influential in making Slaves under the control of their masters. He has been known to possess humans.

Kobal: (Christian Demonology) He is an arch-demon who is, the patron of comedians and the Entertainment Director of Hell. Not surprisingly, his demon form has been seen in Las Vegas. He is described as a pinkish color skin, and tusk like teeth. He has a talent for getting crowds to gather, and has been known to "stalk" the talent to get them to perform in Hell. If he doesn't get his way, it is said the talent ends up dying albeit drug overdose, plane crash or anything, but right after they have committed enough sin, to get them into Hell.

Kok-Lir: (Christian Demonology) His past is not that well known. He has been taunting people in big cities for centuries, because he likes to hang around trash dumpsters and feast on vermin. When a human happens to cross the threshold to dispose of waste, he appears. He is described as a squid-like, blue skinned "monster." If you don't turn around it is assumed that he kills you and dumps what is left in the dumpster. (this theory is only because of cases in which people have carried their trash out, and never came back, but were found "chewed up" in the dumpster.)

Kolga: (Nordic Demonology) Daughter of Aegir and Ran, she has long since become more evil once Jehovah took power. She has been a known concubine of Satan himself. Said to occasionally possess a human, and has a love for doing so on cruise ships.

Kosh: (Slavic Demonology) He is known to inhabit the forest along the Milcov River. He has a talent for attacking those who are lost or away from home. Some blame the werewolf legend on him, due to his human-wolf hybrid appearance. Some have actually said that he has bitten people and caused others to change to his appearance, however I find this to be nothing more than folk-lore.

Kostchtchie: (Slavic Demonology) Also known as Koschei the Deathless or Demon of death. A demon of Russian religious mythos, a goblin of death. This horrid monster is described as having a death's head and fleshless skeleton, "through which is seen the black hood flowing and the yellow heart beating." He is armed with an iron staff, with which he knocks down all who come in his path. In spite of his ugliness, he is said to be a great admirer of young girls and women. He is avaricious, hates old and young alike, and particularly those who are fortunate. His dwelling is amongst the mountains of the Koskels and the Caucasus, and will venture from there on occasion to the cities to wreak havoc. He was spotted during the time of Rasputin and supposedly slaughtered anyone who stood in the way of him from being near the royals.

L

Lebara: (Mayan Demonology) A Mayan demon still worshipped by the cult of Yoruban, to this day. We do know there are still sacrifices, including human made and that the cult is known to include people on "secret duty" in the local governments in Brazil, Mexico, Columbia and Panama.

Legba: (Christian Demonology) He is known as the guardian demon of crossroads, In the old wise take about the person who wishes to finally make the deal with the devil, they go to the crossroads, (there have been reports of at least 4 sets on every continent on the planet, except Antarctica) And wait, at midnight Legba will appear and hear the persons wish. If Legba deems the person to not be a threat and that they are sincere about their pact, he will take the person to see Satan for the deal.

Leonard: (Christian Demonology) Known in Germany as Urian, he is the Inspector General of Black Magic and Sorcery. He is a first order demon, Inspector, Master of the Sabbaths. He presided over these as a great black goat with three horns and the head of a fox. There were reports of when Hitler was investigating the Occult he tried to have his Mages and Shamans conjure Urian (Leonard) so serve as a diplomatic status to the Nazi Regime.

Leraje: (Christian Demonology) also known as Larajie, Leraie, and Leraikka. This demon is used for ritual battles. Leraie A great marquis of Hell. He commands thirty of the infernal legions. He comes in the likeness of an archer, clad in green, and bearing bow and quiver. He occasions battles and causes arrow wounds to putrefy. He is known to have a fondness for both dark and light. *(See seal symbols on next page)*

Daytime calling seal of Leraje

Nighttime calling seal of Leraje

Leviathan: (Mixed Demonology) The androgynous Grand Admiral of Hell who is supposed to have seduced Adam and Eve. Dragon of the Sea, the Crooked Serpent of the abyss In the Bible, one of the names of the primeval dragon subdued by Jehovah at the outset of creation: "You crushed Leviathan's heads, gave him as food to the wild animals" (Psalm 74:14; see also Isaiah 27:1; Job 3:8; Amos 9:3). Biblical writers also refer to the dragon as Rahab (Job 9:13; Psalm 89:10) or simply as the Abyss (Habakkuk 3:10). Leviathan was the enormous whale who appeared throughout the legends of the Hebrews. He was the demon master of the ocean, and reigned also as king of beasts, feared by God and men alike. No man-made weapons could hurt him. It is thought that he is derived from the Canaanite Lotan, and that he is related to the Babylonian Tiamat and the Greek Hydra. Descriptions of him say he had seven heads. According to the medieval hierarchies he was the Grand Admiral of the maritime regions of Hell. He is perhaps best known from the Biblical tale in the Book of Jonah. Jonah had fled in fear of God towards the city of Tarshish which lay across the sea. But during the sea journey, God created a mighty tempest. The ship's crew found out that Jonah was the cause of the story; they threw him overboard, and he was swallowed by Leviathan. Gabriel will fight against Leviathan and overcome. Of course, in Psalms 74:26 God is praised as having crushed the heads of Leviathan: "it was You who crushed the heads of Leviathan, who left him as food for the denizens of the desert"

After the severed breakdown of the way the pantheons were finally decoded and worked out, Leviathan was discovered to merely be a very powerful Demon, however not Satan Himself. And of course finding out that Gabriel did not "slay the beast" as it was written was to some discomfort as well. We know that Leviathan is in purgatory, and that as there have been attempts to unleash him, it might require some serious psychic energy in order to do so.

Lilith:(Christian Demonology) The first wife of Adam, before Eve, who in Jewish folklore, a demoness that is an enemy of newborn children. The name Lilith is etymologically related to the Sumerian word lil (wind), not to the Hebrew word laylah (night), as was long supposed. Like the Sumerian wind demon and its later Babylonian counterpart, Lilith is regarded as a succubus. In the popular imagination, Lilith eventually became confused with Lamashtu, the Babylonian child-slaying demon. In Isaiah 34:14, in which she is depicted as a demon of the desert. There are other references beyond this. We know after the 3rd holy war she took refuge from Allah and Jehovah and became a bride of Satan, to which she serves even though she has a strong will and has vowed never to have a man have power over her (mainly the reason why Allah in particular wants her destroyed or cast into purgatory.) We do know she does possess humans on occasion, and has been known to temp women, Muslim in particular into denying their husbands wishes. She adorns

herself with many ornaments like a despicable harlot, and takes up her position at the crossroads to seduce the sons of man.
When a fool approaches her, she grabs him, kisses him, and pours him wine of dregs of vipers' gall.

When she sees that he is gone astray after her from the path of truth, she divests herself of all ornaments which she put on for that fool. Her ornaments are: her hair is long and red like a rose, her cheeks are white and red, from her ears hang six ornaments, Egyptian cords and all the ornaments from the land of the East hang from her nape. Her mouth is set like a narrow door comely in its decor, her tongue is sharp like a sword, her words are smooth like oil, her lips are red like a rose and sweetened by all the sweetness of the world. Even today, among the Jews of Palestine, Lilith - succubus, child stealer and evil eye - is averted from the bed by hanging over it a charm in Hebrew. It is made of special Kabalistic paper and tied together with a piece of rue, garlic, and a fragment of a mirror. Furthermore, in medieval times, Lilith was considered the cause of nocturnal emissions and was believed to be a dangerous presence in the marital chamber.

Lilitu: (Kabbalah Demonology) An ancient demon connected with Lilith, as she is Liliths daughter from her marriage with Adam. Order of the ancients, she is a demon that helps. It is said that she was born when Lilith was away from Adam, and that Lilitu came to see her father when she was 10 and was denied by him. She pleaded and Adam was beset on not acknowledging his daughter, so followed in her mother's footsteps and left. But then for some time she even left the Earthen Realm, and lived in hell with her mother until the 4th holy war, where upon she had even become bored with the demonic way. It is said that she finds those in need and helps them.

Lima: (Christian Demonology) A demon god worshipped in Haiti. He is said to be prone to liking rum and sugar. And he will strike upon newcomers who strike upon the people born upon the land. His sister Lingelson is said to protect from above, while Lima protects from the lowlands.

Lingelson: (Christian Demonology) A demon worshipped in Haiti, does not like children of foreigners. Her brother Lima, is said to protect the lowlands, while she protects from the heavens.

Lucibel:(Christian Demonology) Name given to Lucifer before the fall, most people do not realize the complete story of the second holy war in which Lucifer tried to over throw the powers of Jehovah. This went on for what can be described as three human years. During this time when Lucifer was considered an enemy, but not cast out of heaven, He was referred to as Lucibel, and transformed into the first demon. As Jehovah thought he might still have some good in him, and there might be the possibility of redemption. Though shortly before the end of the war, Allah tried to gain his throne and in effort to deal with Allah, Jehovah cast Lucibel from the heavens in order to create an enemy for Allah (Jehovah's thinking was along the lines, that Allah would not only have to fight Jehovah, but Lucibel, and Jehovah was right.)

Lucifer:(Christian Demonology) Light bearer, son of the morning; former seraphim cast out of heaven, Lucifer/Satan/The Devil Often misconstrued as being Satan, as they are two separate demons, though Lucifer no longer exist, as his given name at the time of his fall was Lucibel. Lucifer, was the true angelic version of the being, when he became Lucibel, he in fact became a demon. When he was cast from the heaven pantheon, he absorbed the power of 12 lower demons, even a few deities. Lucibel crept into the Muslim pantheon and took power from Allah (Which was Jehovah's wishes, though

Satan did not know It.) and later, Lucibel in a great show of power announced himself the prince of darkness, and took commanded from Hades of the underworld. He declared Hell his land, and even cast energy shields around Hell so that no one under Zeus, Ra, Jehovah nor Allah could pass into. He formed the many legions of demons, and was bent on not destroying man as it was destroying the Gods, by destroying man. Some have theorized that it was Satan who tried to temp Jehovah's son, Jesus during the crucifixion, however evidence points that it was in fact Satan taking on Lucibel's form.

Lucifuge:(Mixed Demonology) Also known as Lucifuge Rofocale, he is the Prime Minister of the demons of Hell. He is served by Baal and Aguares. He serves Satan as his lord, as he is equal to Adam, and has power over all the treasures of the world. He is a known possesser of humans and he avoids light, and can only assume a body at night.

Lusx:(Christian Demonology) A demon known for his hate of farmers, as he will destroy crops, and cause livestock to die. He does not like to see man gain wealth, (and farming is the key step, because without a wealth of food, man would spend more time worrying about what to grow instead of making money to live and purchase from farmers.) so he loves to see this step removed to crush mans spirit and wealth.

Lucex: (Christian Demonology) A demon, known to inhabit beaches, (most recently as of 2011, in Daytona Beach, Florida.) likes to perform incubus acts on young females. Which of course is completely disturbing to women, as if being raped alone wasn't hard enough, imagine being raped while your attacker is invisible and even in the twilight. In some including the most recent case of attack, semen discharge has even been found. Which of course causes law enforcement to try and cover up the situation, (how to you track DNA back to a human, when the DNA cannot be mapped?) as reports might cause a panic and slow the tourist trade in the area as most areas with beaches, rely on tourism.

M

Maleficia: (Mixed Demonology) This demon is not used internally, but is used when casting spells to hurt others. He is said to be a demon who gains power and contributes power to those seeking revenge. During the beginning reign of Jehhovah, this demon was under Egyptian rule, and was employed to punish disobedient slaves.

Malphas: (Christian Demonology) He appears as a raven Grand President of Hell, commander of forty legions. He builds impregnable citadels and towers, overthrows the Temples and Towers of his enemies, finds good workmen, gives familiar spirits, receives sacrifices and deceives the sacrificers. He is depicted as a crow with a hoarse voice, though will assume human form if commanded.

Mammon: (Christian Demonology) The Demon of Avarice (greed), he is known in most pantheons; however is almost an arch-demon as he does not play a role in positive nor negative thought. He is ruled by that in which he rules, greed.

Manuval: (Mixed Demonology) She is known to currently be in the mid-western United States as of 2009. She is described as taking two forms. One of a human female, with red hair and attractive by the reports. And the second is her demonic form. Her demonic form is almost that of human; however her skin is described as "reptilian blue" and she has micro horns protruding in a circle around her face. Her exact origins are unknown. The earliest reports are made from the 12th century in which she was seen as royalty in France. She is known to make her way into most in the modern world with money. She is believed to merely be a "gold digger" and serves no exact side other than hers. She has been linked to A. Crowley during his younger years, and has even been linked to Gerald Gardner. The rumor is, "if you have money are wanting to perform magick then maybe Manuval will pay you a visit."

Mara: (Asian Demonology) He is demon who attempts to trick a follower into damning their soul. He is described as almost "Muhammad like" in appearance. Some are actually saying that he is the demon which causes those who follow Allah to perform suicide acts.

Marax: (Christian Demonology) This demon helps the Mothers-of-Darkness understand astrology. A Mother will lose her powers if he is removed from her mind. He is capable of being split into a billion pieces and a small part of him can enable the worst of seers to double if not triple their psychic powers.

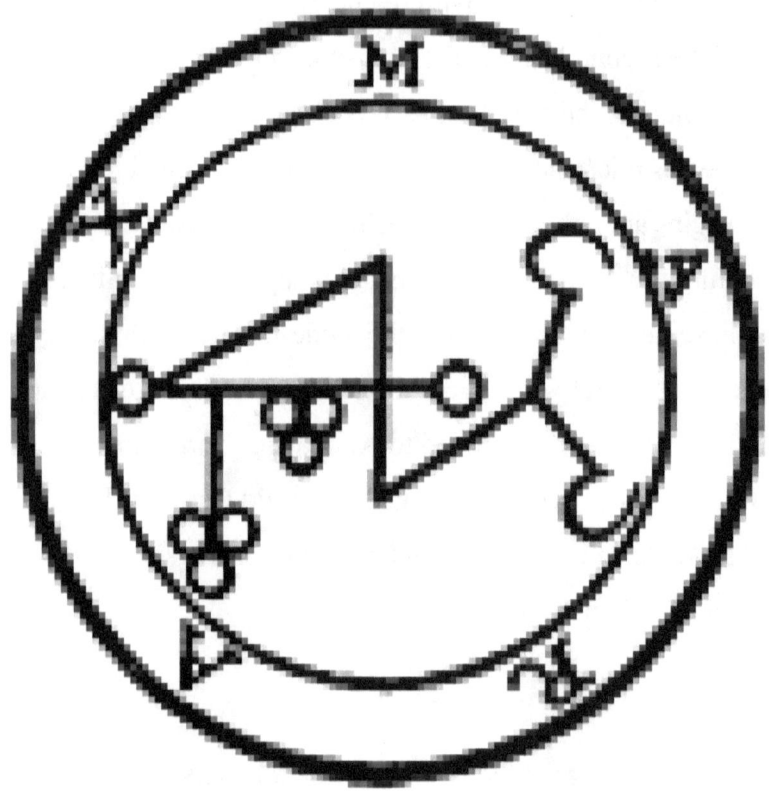

Mastema: (Kabbalah Demonology) The leader of the offspring of fallen angels. Leader of fallen angels whose job is to tempt men to sin and accuse them before God Leader of human/demon offspring. Mastema is mentioned only in The Book of Jubilees and in the

Fragments of a Zadokite Work. In the Book of Jubilees, Mastema seems to be identified with Satan. He asked the Lord that some of the spirits might be allowed to remain with him to do his will. God granted his request and allowed one tenth of the spirits to remain with Mastema, while the other nine parts would be condemned. He seems to be of a different nature than those evil spirits he is pleading for. He has no concern that he will be bound with the others. This is similar to the chief Satan and his class of Satans (see 1 Enoch 40:7). Jubilees implies that Mastema is subservient to God. His task is simply to tempt men to sin and if they do, he accuses them before the Throne of God. He does not initiate the process of sin, but Mastema and his spirits then lead them on to greater wrongdoing. This is related to the Biblical function of Satan, where men can achieve righteousness if they are tempted and resist.

Melchom: (Mixed Demonology) A treasurer of Hell, he is obsessively counting the wealth and has no apparent tolerance for thievery, upon the wealth of Hell. (Ironic, because stealing being a sin, causes thieves to go to Hell.) If a thief is caught, he will not stop at nothing to have that soul dissolved or at least sent to purgatory.

Mephistopheles: (Christian Demonology) He sometimes is described as a servant of the Devil, and other times is a name for

Satan himself. His name was another name for the devil in the middle Ages, However when certain volumes came to light about his role, we have found out, that he is in fact Satan's son. We know he takes on the typical form of "horned devil" and has been found to be the lover to the Nordic deity Loki.

Merihim: (Christian Demonology) He is sometimes referred too as "The Prince of Pestilence", known for causing insects to overwhelm a community, to which he has a massive talent. He is known to cause insects to completely take over any city, the only way to get rid of him is to either pray for a massive cold front to flow through (To which it is best to reduce your heat in your home or the insects may go there) or to line your property with a mixture of salt, vinegar, lilac and lavender.

Mictain: (Aztec Demonology) God of death, later when Jehovah took over the main Pantheons from the other Gods, he made Micatin an arch-demon. He is posted to the gate on East heaven and is considered the transporter demon to Hell's Gate, for that region.

Moko-Titi: (Japanese Demonology) A hideous lizard demon, known for his willingness to destroy entire families at once.

Moloch:(Kabbalah Demonology) He was worshipped by the Israelites through child sacrifice. In the Old Testament, Moloch was an evil deity called the 'abomination of the Ammonites.' Worshipped as a sun god, Moloch embodied the savage and devastating aspects of the sun's heat. He was also thought to be the bringer of plagues. The Ammonites erected huge bronze statues in his honor, depicting him as a bull-headed colossus with extremely long arms, sitting on a throne of brass. His rites included human sacrifices, especially the immolation of firstborn infants. This sacrifice was said to be the most powerful way to avert disaster and death from the community at large.

Morax:(Christian Demonology) A great earl and a president of Hell, who appears like a human-headed bull, and gives skill in astronomy with good familiars. He knows the virtues of all herbs and precious stones. He has command of thirty-six of the infernal legions.

Mothman:(Mixed Demonology) See listing for Reftu.

Mullin:(Christian Demonology) Lieutenant to Leonard, and even served as his diplomat to Hitler during World War 2. Some theorize it was ultimately Mullin's decisions that did not grant Hitler supreme occult power during this time, and the reason for Hitler in turn losing the war. Mullin is said to be the one who suggested the Holocaust, as Mullin is also an arch-demon, to Allah.

Murmur: (Mixed Demonology) Great Duke, comes with trumpets sounding and rules 30 legions This demon is in charge of the soul. He is connected to core issues. A great duke and earl, appears in the form of a soldier riding on a griffin, and having a duke's crown on his head. He is preceded by two ministers sounding trumpets. He teaches philosophy perfectly, and constrains the souls of the dead to appear and to answer questions. He was partly of the Order of Thrones and partly of Angels. *(See seal symbol on next page)*

Seal of MurMur

Mush: (Christian Demonology) A demon of eclipses, darkness, and known for his candidacy in making humans, "afraid of the dark when they are children. He is described as a small demon, about 4 feet in height, with a brownish, leathery skin. (These reports cannot be taken as complete fact as he has never been seen in the light.)

N

Naburus: (Christian Demonology) Also known as Naberios, Naburus, Naberius A Marquis of Hell who has connections to Cerberus. He is a strong demon in charge of 29 legions, a Marquis of hell, - Protector of the gates of hell. Associated with Cerberus, out of the Greek Mythos, he in his demonic form is a few steps removed. Once Zeus turned over the main pantheon to Jehovah, Jehovah began realigning Gods, Demigods and titans into his own ideas of what would encourage people to follow his reign of power. He saw Naburus, and even though his previous form was actually just a guard who patrolled along the River Styx, Jehovah saw potential. Naburus is described as one of the few demons who is loving. And he encourages his legions to be that way as well. He is depicted as a crow with a hoarse voice that gives skill in arts and sciences, especially rhetoric, and restores lost dignities and honors.

Namtar: (Sumerian Demonology) A minor god in the underworld in Sumerian mythology, Namtar, was regarded as the bringer of disease and pestilence. It is fate, destiny in its evil aspect, pictured as a demon of the underworld. In addition to spreading disease, Namtar acted as the herald or messenger and chief minister of Ereshkigal, the queen of the Sumerian underworld, and the god Nergal. Nergal in his guise as the god Irra, and Namtar were believed to cause all diseases in mortals.

Nard: (Egyptian Demonology) He is Ra's number one security, officer. A post which he still serves to this day under Ra in the ever realms of the past. He sometimes escapes and makes his presence known to humans (As do most in the original mythos.) He will appear in either his human form or his demonic form. His human form is simple, no matter what he always has one eye that takes a cat's eye appearance. (The way to catch him is notice one eye may switch with the "cat's eye" appearance.) In his demonic form, he is described as the size of a horse; however he is a large lion. On the tip of his tail is the head of a snake (Which some have described his tail as a large snake, however the most recent report in 2004 states it was merely the head.)

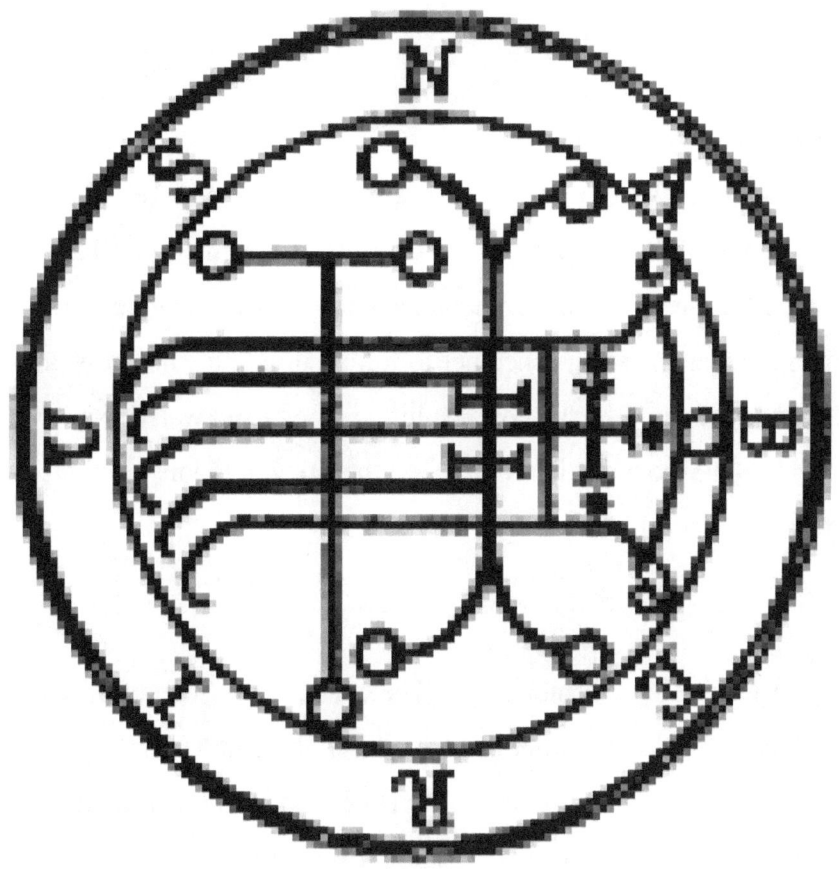

Nask: (Christian Demonology) Arch Demon, turned his back on Satan shortly before Christ was born.

They believe that it was Nask who freed the early Jews and Christians whenever they were locked up for their beliefs. Some have wondered is Nask is still an Angel, however the records from the early holy Wars show that Nask was once an angel who turned his back on Jehovah.

Natasha: (Christian Demonology) Another of Satan's demon wives. Some say the newest in fact. We know that she was once a concubine of Cernunnos, the Druid God. After the other gods had had their time in the main pantheon, Natasha was wanting be worshipped again. Satan asked her to follow him to the meadow, and before had Cernunnos staged to be in the woods and watched in horror as Satan seduced her and sealed their new relationship right there on the spot.

Nergal: (Babylonian Demonology) The Chief of the Secret Police of Hell. Under the second order of Satan, he is also known as the demigod Nergal, God of underworld. He is a second order demon who is an associate of Beelzebub. Nergal was originally a Sumerian deity before being demonized by the Europeans theologians.

Nicor: (Nordic Demonology) Water demon known for drowning humans; can cause hurricanes, tempests and the like. Some have said the ships that came to the rescue of the ill-fated passenger ship Titanic, they spotted Nicor lurk by the infamous Iceberg. (If you look at historical accounts for a picture of the infamous iceberg, the photographer, Stephan Rehorek stated later that he had taken the picture because it had "red paint" on the side of it. He admitted later in life that he had seen a creature by the waterline, he described it as a creature that was a "dark blue, if not black in color, and had the head which looked like a centipede that should be 100 feet long" Judging by that description, it would appear that Nicor was in the area, and made sure the iceberg was right in path with the vessel.)

Nybbas: (Mixed Demonology) Manager of visions and dreams, inferior order charlatan. An odd demon who apparently loves human interaction. He is mostly seen in his human form, however few have seen his demonic form as well. His human form is described as a rather handsome male, blond hair and very polite (Of course this is an act.) his demonic form is a bit formed as he looks like what most would describe as a the Grim Reaper. He takes on more of a skeletal look with eyes. He has surprised most with his schemes. He has bilked monies from those in dire needs, churches, and charities.

Nybras:(Mixed Demonology) An demon who publicizes the pleasures of hell. She is known to hang around at bars that cater to the BDSM crowds. (For those who do not know or are familiar, yes that is the whole "whips and chains" thing.) She looks for those who really have a love for being tortured. After all they have "safe words" and so forth. But she will get into a person's life, and influence the person to commit just enough sin, then call for others to take the life of the person before they have a chance to follow Christian Doctrine and "repent." Find a person carrying the satanic bible, and you will see Nybras follow them. She loves to talk about the joys of pleasures, and has found those influenced with their philosophies to be the easiest of her targets. Though she is known for challenges, she will walk into a church group and find prey there as well. (I would like to point out, to the Satanist reading, that yes I understand the principals behind your belief and in no way am trying to insult. I am merely restating the known knowledge.)

Nysrogh:(Christian Demonology) An inferior demon, second order demon, chief of the house of princesses and known to actually have distaste for demonic service to any overlord, she is very much into trying to blend into living with humans, and as some who have encountered her consider her to be nothing more than a "spoiled brat". She has tried to blend in with humans so she can game fame, however she does know that any mass fame could cause her identity to be known and in turn she will eventually stop thinking about becoming famous for a while, as she knows that if she is discovered amongst humans there is a good chance she will be forced back into a Hell Pantheon for some time.

Nyx: (Christian Demonology) The sister and wife of Erebus. Together they are a constant thorn in the side of married couples. Though they are married themselves they both work in their own way to split couples up before they have had a chance to combine and make offspring. Daughter of chaos,

Nysrock: (Christian Demonology). Second order demon, who is chief of staff in the main royal palace in the palace center of hell. He was once under the rule of Hades when Hell itself had his namesake, however after Jehovah came to power and of course the incidents in which Satan came to rule over hell, Nysrock took his position as the chief of staff in the main royal palace. Now, there is a report that his assistant, Zlothos, a newer demon, was once known as a human, Adolph Hitler.

O

Olisha: (Mixed Demonology) An evil demon goddess from Haiti, she is a favorite of voodoo and black magic users from the region. In Christian lore, she has become a bit of a staple as the demon that makes women falter in their marriages.

Orgeuil: (Christian Demonology) One of the two demons said to have been successfully exorcised from Elisabeth Allier in 1639 by Francois Faconnet. The two demons who had possessed her for twenty years admitted that they had entered her body by means of a crust of bread they had put into her mouth when she was seven years old. They fled from her body in the presence of the Holy Sacrament. The name of the other demon was Bonifarce.

Oriax: (Christian Demonology) She is a Duchess, and a demon who commands 30 legions. He teaches astrology to those who seek the knowledge. His origins are from Egyptian mythos. Though she has been seen around the planet and he has been still sighted in the lands along the Nile. She is sister to Orias.

DEMONOLOGY 101

Orias: (Christian Demonology) He is the demon of divination, and a great marquis of hell. He appears in the form of a lion bestriding a strong horse; he has a serpent's tail, and holds two enormous hissing snakes in his right hand. He teaches the virtues of the planets and the mansions thereof; he transforms men, gives dignities, prelates, and confirmations, with the favor of friends and foes. He is also the demon of divination. He is brother of Oriax.

Ornias: (Christian Demonology) The name of a harassing demon, He is known to have a demonic form that is said to be almost human, however he does have some tell tale signs. His palms have his other two eyes (one each per palm.) He is known to harass the elderly, and likes to "swindle" them.

Oroan: (African/ Tribal Demonology) The Guyana demon of suicides and death, I find this one really interesting, as a group of his followers were just mere miles from Jonestown, and the members of Jonestown were known to harass them. Supposedly Jim Jones himself made an appearance in their village, known as Oroantrone. Shortly after Jones appearance to inform them about the "power of the lord" the Jonestown massacre took place just days later. I am not trying to dismiss Jones's madness off as case of a religious war, however it does shed some light possibly on the situation.

Orthon:
(Kabbalah Demonology) A demon of unknown origin who is said to have ties with possessions in France and with the Masonic order of

Palladinism in 19th century Italy. Some demonologists have concluded that the demon is associated with the Illuminati's private order of Masonic officers.

Orusula: (Christian Demonology) Costa Rican demon that appears in the form of a giant pig, his foam gives people a fatal rash. This is actually one that baffles me, as I have spoken to some of his victims friends and relatives, however no one has no knowledge of his origins, let alone true research that can be found. If you are in Costa Rica, just avoid pigs I recommend.

Ose: (Christian Demonology) A great president, appears at first like a leopard, and then in human form. He gives skill in all liberal sciences, and true answers concerning divine and secret things. He can change men into any shape that the exorcist may desire, and he that is changed will not know it. He governs 30 legions in hell.

P

Paimon: (Kabbalah Demonology) This knight spirit is very obedient to Satanis, and is used as an enforcer in an internal system. He continues to report back as to whether the internal worlds are intact or not. He has been known to possess humans, and was last reported to do so in 2010. *(See seal symbol on next page)*

Seal of Paimon

Pan: (Celtic Demonology) Once considered the God of lust, he chose to remain on the side of Man. Most Christians deem him evil because he denies Jehovah praise, but some have suggested that is just Pans way. It does make sense that Pan would be on the side of Man and not deity, as Lust can be a powerful tool, and to leave a deity in charge of it does make one worried over how mankind would garner a driving force in humans to achieve their goals. (Sex can be quite a motivator you know?)

Panmor: (Mixed Demonology) The most part of Panmor that most scholars can review and say about this demon is that she has had a knack at keeping herself with the top niche of whoever is in power. She is described almost as faerie based demonic presence. She is known to be considered by an arch-demon as in the fact she only goes for her own side in situations, regardless however of who is in charge of the Underworld. She can take a human form that is known to have the faerie look to herself when she does so (Short, pixie type hair.) She has a talent for scheming humans into what can only be described as life altering events such as, cheating on one's spouse, making idiot business dealings (to which she is usually the benefactor) and has been known to use herself as a way to alter ones perceptions on religions

Paymon: (Christian Demonology) This demon governs 200 legions in Hell. He is known as one for diplomacy and has a great aptitude at public speaking. When those paranoid about public leaders such as Presidents worshipping the devil, this is the specific demon they worship in order to gain the talent of a public tongue. This is very ironic, as his symbol has been seen to be in very high public places such as the White House. However to those who believe this to be so, should remember that the worship of him is very hard to do without getting caught. Might I remind you that his symbol follows very deep Christian symbolism, (the true Satanic Cross is very similar to the Christian one, only Hollywood uses the "upside down" cross, as the true Satanic Cross only features some wording as its difference to the Christian Cross. I personally believe this for the Christians to be shortsightedness, as the cross was originally a Pagan symbol, as Jesus was crucified on Scaffolding, not a Cross as the mythos would lead you to believe.) And it is with this symbol, the speaker may gain his or her power.

Pazuzu: (Sumerian Demonology) A winged demon, feared by the people of ancient Mesopotamia, It is a creature with a deformed head, the wings of an eagle, the sharp claws of a lion on its hands and feet, and the tail of a scorpion. The Mesopotamians believed that

Pazuzu lived in the desert, and was the focal point of the film the Exorcist. It should be noted that in the original case, of which the film was based, the boy in St. Louis was possessed by Pazuzu. This case in the 1950s was recorded and that was the very case that William Peter Blatty based his novel and the film was based upon. Others have wondered is Pazuzu had indeed began possessing humans after that case, only after recorded incidents in 1998 and 2004 do we know for a fact that Pazuzu has indeed been behind human possession.

Phenex:(Mixed Demonology) This demon is a poet who speaks to exorcists but supposedly does not need to obey exorcists. He is a great marquis in Western Hell and he appears like the bird of that name, singing dulcet tones in a child's voice. When he assumes human shape at the will of the Sorcerer, he speaks marvelously of all sciences, proves an excellent poet, and fulfills orders admirably. He hopes to return to the Seventh Throne in 1200 years, after man and god are on their final war.

Philatanus: (Christian Demonology) He is also known as Philotanus. This is a second order demon in service to Belial. He tempts mortals to engage in sodomy and pedophile behaviors, it is said whenever an adult reflects on their childhood if they were sexually abused, then Philatanus grows in his power to temp others. There are those in the Kabbalah faith that believe that he gains strength of of a child's tears. I personally feel that either way he is not only a demon to shun, but one that should be destroyed if given that chance.

Pickullus: (Mixed demonology) She is known as a messenger demon. She is one of the few that can transverse into all known pantheons of realms that any of the gods inhabitant. She even according to records has the ability to transverse into purgatory. Most conjurers call upon her to deliver messages to other realms, as well do the gods.

Pitkus: (Slavic Demonology) Once known as the God of the Night, He later became the demon of the night, after the last few pantheons ruled by Jehovah came to power. He is known to roam the shadows, and scare people who are alone in the darkness. However, he does not scare or frighten for pleasure, it is said that he does so to protect the humans from other beings that roam the darkness.

Pitua: (Asian Demonology) A demon in Maori myth, is known try and destroy to old men, who are usually widowers. Is known to take human form of that of a male with green eyes, and will stop at nothing if his target is you.

Procel: (Mixed demonology) This demon appears in the form of an angel, and has complete power over water, to the point he can make it boil or freeze solid at will. He speaks mystically of hidden things, teaches geometry and the liberal sciences, and at the command of the operator will make a great commotion like that of running waters. He was of the Order of the Powers before his fall. Most do not know if his origins are that of Sumerian or Mesopotamians, but there is one record in which he froze the water for Jesus to walk upon and shortly after that, Allah disbanded him into demon-ship because Allah was beginning his war with Jehovah.

Proserpine: (Greek Demonology) also known as Persephone. Once the Goddess of the Underworld, she is now sometimes known as a princess of Hell. It is said she possesses great beauty and when Satan took his throne over the underworld, he tried to wed her. However Proserpine's father, Hades did not like this union and forbid it. Satan did try to bed her down, but she was repulsed by him, (you have to remember just because the underworld was the underworld, it did not mean beings had to "be ugly".) so when Satan tried to trick her into his bed, she cut out his heart and brought it before Jehovah, who in turn granted her permanent passage to the kingdoms of the higher lands. She is known to travel through our world from time to time, and loves to cause muse like thoughts in that of women.

Pruflas:(Christian Demonology) He reigned in Babylonia where he had the head of an owl. He stirs up strife, starts wars, initiates quarrels and reduces people to mendacity. He gives lengthy answers to all questions. Now, under the reign of Satan he is commander of twenty-six legions, and is considered an excellent tactician.

Purson:(Christian Demonology) This demon blows internal trumpets, and is believed connected to the revelator to the Anti-Christ. He also knows the systems of how certain mythos can defeat the other mythos. Satan, Allah and even Jehovah and Zeus have tried to get Purson to tell them the information to destroy each other from time, to time. But during the Greek reign, Purson was faithful to his goddess mother, Eris. And with that, it is done. However he has been known to give humans the sacred information's for a small fee. Some believe it is because he thinks humans should have more power than they were given.

Pwcca: (Druidic Demonology) Also known as Pooka. In the Druidic, and eventually in the Celtic mythos, he was known as lord of the underworld. After the beginning of the Holy Wars, he assumed his position in the 3rd level of hell.

Pytho: (Mixed Demonology) He is known as a demon of lies, and has been seen primarily as a serpent. It is suggested he is a rather large serpent and that is where the name Python comes from. He can assume human form, and it has not been fully conformed, but there has been evidence as to linking him to Titan, Medusa, as he is her offspring.

Q

Qac:(Kabbalah Demonology) This demon of unknown specific origins is known to become enabled from sunrise to sunset. His brother, Qad, however is known to inhabit the time from sunset to sunrise. It is believed from certain reports that they are in fact the same being, just possessing the same space. They are known to be a lover of trickery when it comes to children. To give an example, they are the ones who tempt a crook to carjack a car without knowledge of a child being in the back seat. The swell in power the more a child is in danger.

Qad:(Kabbalah Demonology) The demon brother of Qac (See

above.) Known to inhabit the planet, from time of sunset to sunrise.

Qah: (Mixed demonology) Assistant to Xax, Demon of the order of pain. Qah is known to love his assignments when he temps humans and animals into torture. There has been a lot of links to Qah and torture by razors.

Qanel:
(Kabbalah Demonology) This demon, known to appear in form of a human sized body with the wings of a sparrow and the head of a goat, has a great love of robbery. He has been spotted by banks and such, and not surprisingly those very banks end up being robbed. Some say he can transform himself into a true human form, and in cases where humans are caught for bank robbery and the other party involved are not found or caught, the caught suspect always report the "one that got away" was the "one who came up with the idea." As much as I think most bank robbers try to pin the "masterminding" on the other guy, most states charge all involved equally. So to me it does lend value to their claims, especially when another human reports seeing the demon in it's true form, making the escape no less.

Qapb: (Kabbalah Demonology) For some time the profession of this demon was considered a "Secret". However in the 1970s we finally got knowledge. During that time, there was the beginning of the "satanic Panic" in which most Christians and other followers of other faiths, were on the scare of "devil worshippers" who cut babies out of wombs, killed animals and so forth. However the dark forces, knew that if humans were scared over this, they would either grow more paranoid, or begin to work the facts out of lies and lose faith in their religious beliefs all together. Either way the dark forces would win if humans did so. One of the last known incidents in which Qapb had a part to play was in the McMartin Pre-School case. For those unfamiliar, the McMartin Family of Manhattan Beach, California was accused of hundreds of cases of child abuse, both sexual and ritualistic in nature. The family and all parties were completely absolved of those cases, as the evidence was discovered to be contrived by both a child psychologist, Kee MacFarlane who merely stated child sexual abuse in every child she had in her care (Including other children whom had nothing to do with the case,) and by a deranged, mental health patient Judy Johnson, whom had stopped her medications because of her recent divorce (Also should be noted that this woman had also stated the then President, Ronald Regan had molested her children as well.) In the end , even the Child Psychologist, MacFarlane was considered the worst child psychologist as after videos of her interviews with the children were reviewed and shown she had used "strong suggestion" to the children, and the mother Judy Johnson was diagnosed with and hospitalized for acute paranoid schizophrenia and in 1986 was found dead in her home from complications of chronic alcoholism before the preliminary hearing concluded. Now ironically there are those who will still say that "well it just shows the Satanic Conspiracy is large enough to cover it all up," much like those who try to defend the stories of Mike Warnke from the early 1970s, (Who was debunked via The Cornerstone Magazine, a Christian publication, in 1991.) However, when you weigh the facts with common sense, let alone the knowledge of Qapb, and his duties, the picture becomes more clear. He is known to prey on the weak willed and mentally ill.

QstrSur: (Celtic Demonology) This demon is a powerful one, it is known he loves to make places appear haunted and when the humans think it is a ghost or poltergeist, they usually garner the use of a psychic, or a person who is sensitive to psychic power, then he likes to really play. He will cause you to leave your home, even your possessions behind.

Quab: (Mixed demonology) Also known as Q, this demon has no correct shape, it may appear as a human male, or female and any form it deems to be fit. Quab is known as a prankster and loves to torment humans into change their ways of thinking, and doing things. It should be noted, that because Quab has sometimes gone by the name Q since the 11th century, (It is said to call aloud the name Quab to much, that Quab will come forward,) that Freemason Gene

Roddenberry cast the concept of Q in the Star Trek The Next Generation Series, though there are similarities and as my own wife likes to remind me that there is an ounce of truth in every work of fiction, I like to consider the role of Q in the series to be an interesting allusion as to what or who Quab is.

Qutrub: (Muslim Demonology) This demon similar to the Islamic Ghul, is a known source of demonic energy that a sorcerer can harness fairly easily. Most who use necromancy and demon conjuring believe that it is because the Qutrub, unlike other spirits was formed by the planet itself and has the ability to generate this life force in which all living beings draw from. It is known that a Qutrub does assume a human look from time to time, which has been reported that takes a rather great deal of energy, and some have even suggested the Qutrub could be a form of "Psychic Vampire" that drains the energies and life-force out of living beings when in human form. Under its normal form however, it bleeds the energies back into the air, to which humans and other living beings absorb and the cycle renews itself.

Quixt:
(Christian Demonology) This demon was once a bride to the God Allah, and when she began to assume her role as a woman was more demanding than that of a male, Allah scolded her to which she left

the heavens and took refuge on Earth. Allah found her and cursed her into human/demonic form. There have been reports of her sightings near the American New England area. It is said she is more about making women empowered rather than even acknowledging a man, however she is known to take human men as her concubines from time to time.

R

Ragnarok: (Mixed Demonology) She is considered to be an Oracle Demon, under the druidic religion, she often was sighted at the oracle tree before it was destroyed by the early Christian/ roman settlers into what was once called Britannia, now called England. It is said if you approach an oak tree (what supposedly the oracle tree was) you can call upon her to give you insight into the future. But because she is now considered a demon, because she refuses to accept Jehovah's rulings, she is known to bless only those with a desire to bring Christianity or Judaism down.

Rahu: (Mixed Demonology) Also known as Abhra-pisacha, the 'demon of the sky,' was a great prince of the Daityas, a race of gigantic demons who warred against the gods. He is well known in Christian demonology, as the demon who after trying to show Satan how powerful he was, once tried to assassinate the son of Jehovah in his 3rd year of life. His name means "to abandon" or "void," hence blackness or having no body. Since his inception of being a demon, he has been known to possess humans from time to time, most notably, the possession case of Gerald Hart in 1989.

Raiden: (Japanese Demonology) Once considered the god of Rai or thunder and lightning, Raiden has made a name for himself, (not because his persona was featured in a successful line of video games,) He is currently being worshipped by a cult in the Aomon region of Japan, and from the most recent reports managed to put on a good show for the visiting Christian missionaries there to "help people over to the power of Jesus". Which would make sense; after all he prevented the Mongols from invading Japan in 1274, to which only three men escaped. The legend and reports state that he is usually found sitting on a cloud he sent forth a shower of lighting arrows upon the invading fleet. Raiden is portrayed as a red demon with sharp claws, carrying a large drum. He is fond of eating human navels. The only protection against him is to hide under a mosquito net.

Rakshasa: (Mixed Demonology) It is described as a demon whose appearance in the least, horrifying. But the concept falls much deeper than just horrifying. Rakshasa was once a king who was human. He liked to torture people before killing them, when he was finally brought forth for his crimes, he cursed the surrounding area near ancient Kalahari dessert in Africa at 70,000 BC. Then roamed through time as a just a source of evil. By the time of 25,000 BC, most had known of Rakshasa as the demon which he is described to this day. Recently in 1998 there was a cult which was known to worship him as the bringer of the modern destruction or "end of days" as some religions refer to it. The most recent reports are that if summoned, he presents the appearance that would give H.P. Lovecraft shakes, and some describe Rakshasa almost Cthulu in appearance.

Raktavija: (Hindu Demonology) The general of the demon army, considered to be the Hindu version of "Judas", we know of his fondness for animal torture and pedophilia. Known to possess humans, including a recent case in Massachusetts, 2004, in which he possessed a 39 year old, married woman named Jo-Ann (last name withheld). She was said to have killed her pet horses and then attempt to molest her son and daughter. Luckily she was stopped and then put through exorcism, however only when the attending priest transferred the conference of energies from catholic/Christian to Hindu, did the exorcism work.

Ran:(Mixed Demonology) She was once the wife of Nordic God Aegir, she was known to use a net to draw sailors of sinking ships to their doom. When the Nordic Pantheon was dropped from its highpoint, she remained to be considered "Evil" and was made demon by the following religions.
She is described as a large deep red, serpent human hybrid, about the size of an elephant. There were thirteen survivors of the Ferry Estonia sinking in 1994 who claimed to have seen her during the events of that evening.

Raum:(Christian Demonology) His origins are completely unknown. We do know he is a count of Hell, appears in the form of a crow, but assumes human shape when bidden. If summoned or conjured he is known to steal treasure and carries it where commanded; he causes love between friends and foes, then when the bond is strong, he unleashes their earlier feelings for each other upon the humans he went after. Finally he is of the Order of the Throne of

Hell; however it is believed that he is close to the bottom of the list in accession. He commands thirty of the infernal legions.

Ravana:(Hindu Demonology) Ravana is probably the best known of all Indian demons. His power and the awe he inspired among the people put him on equal footing with the European Satan. He was lord and master of Rakshasa, to which he puts to tasks whenever possible. He is known to take joy in the displeasure of others, and gains power off of suffering.

Rara:(Slavic Demonology) Not much is fully known about Rara other than she has been described with almost "Vampire-like" qualities. She will take her human form of pale skin, piercing blue eyes and dark hair. Has been known to seduce men and women over the centuries, and a report in 1788 stated she was once human. However in 1977, New York City, there was an updated report that she is demon, however apparently she had a falling out with the dark lords of the underworlds and was cast human with immortality. She does drink blood, however it is because she paralyzes the victims with her gaze, and she does NOT have fangs. She uses a small razor to cut the human victim. She has been known to drain a victim of blood until death, but apparently only in severe cases.

Rard: (Christian Demonology) His profession is considered a secret. He is a known shape shifter and can take human form. His true self can be seen by looking through "salt-glass". And is described looking as a dark grayish blue gargoyle. There have been sightings in London, New York, Washington and Los Angeles all as of recently as 2009, and in 2010 in Petroleum, West Virginia.

Raum: (Christian Demonology) The true background of this demon is not unknown, nor is it known of the mythological settings that which this demon can be defeated and or driven. Though those who have encountered him do believe that he is acceptable to damage by holy water, or moonbeams "blessed" water via witchcraft. He is known to have a fondness for gambling and gamblers, however he likes it when people win, and their life changes for what they seem would be the best, but it almost never works like that. There was a reported case in 1987 in which a man, Todd Dodson claimed that Raum had came to him, and offered to allow him to win at horse racing, so he tried it and sure enough Todd won. Shortly after though, Todd's mother, sister and brother were all killed in a plane crash. Todd's girlfriend died of cancer, and the now known where about of Mr. Dodson are no longer known. Raum is described in human form as around five and a half feet tall, dark hair and green eyes. It is said his left eye twitches uncontrollably.

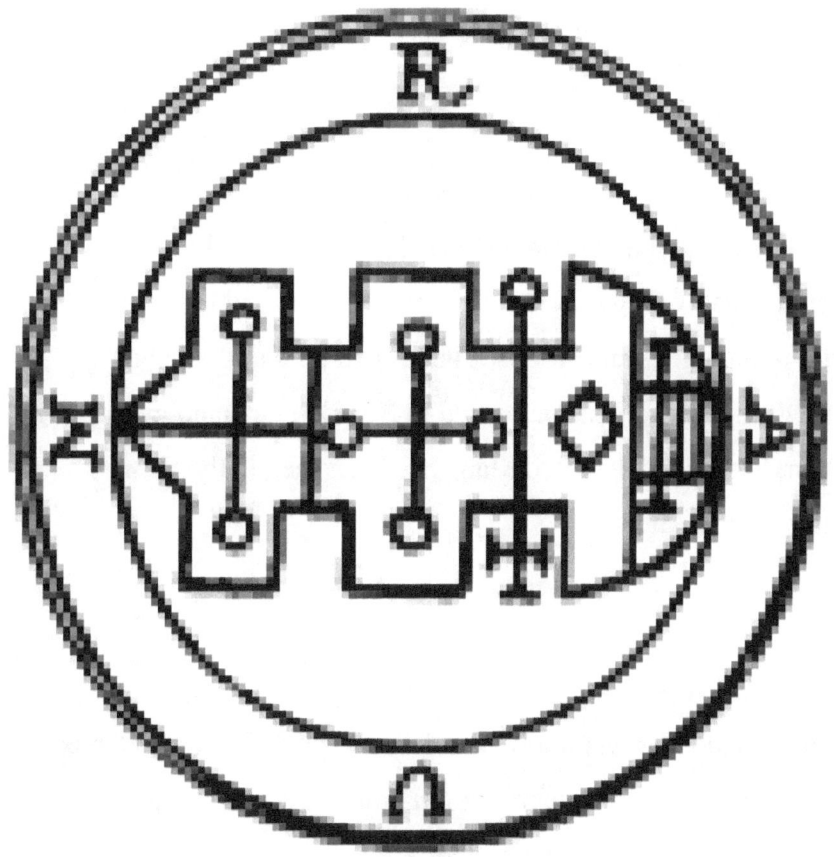

Rdjab:(Mixed Demonology) This demon known to exist before Jehovah later would serve Jehovah then be banished during the 3rd holy war. It is not known if he commands any legions, but it is known that there is a strong hatred of Rdjab by Jehovah.

Red Man:(Christian Demonology) He was supposed to be furious when the rash voyager intruded on his solitude, and to show his anger in the winds and storms. The French peasants believed that a mysterious little red man appeared to Napoleon to announce coming military reverses. The "Red Man" has been seen in the French countryside as late as 1998.

Reftu:(Mixed Demonology) This demon, is also known as the being called Mothman. He is referred to in multiple resources as the giver of information of pending disasters. He is described as a human sized being, covered in fur and the head basically is in the top of the chest. He appears hunched over and has a wingspan of 14 feet. Reftu, has given clues and hints at upcoming disasters. He was most famously known during the collapse of the Silver Bridge in Point Pleasant, WV. However it does not stop there. There have been sightings at such events as 9-11, The Challenger explosion, the

Columbia disaster, Pearl Harbor, the Hindenburg disaster and many aircraft disasters. Reftu has stated there was more of his kind, but none have fully been recorded. He has also admitted through discussions during 2008 he was once considered the "son of a god", though this cannot be confirmed.

Renove: (Christian Demonology) also known as Ronove, she is a demon who assists with demonic speaking in tongues and rhetoric, if there is a riddle, she has been known to have possibly been the muse for it. She likes to show up and confuse anyone she can, especially if it happens to be a life threatening situation. She has a grey/bluish skin color, piercing red eyes and almost a dark royal blue hair. She has a small horn/scale pattern that begins at the base of her skull and proceeds down her back. She is known for taking on humans lovers, but they need to impress her by being quick witted and able to solve some strikingly hard puzzles. *(See seal symbol on next page)*

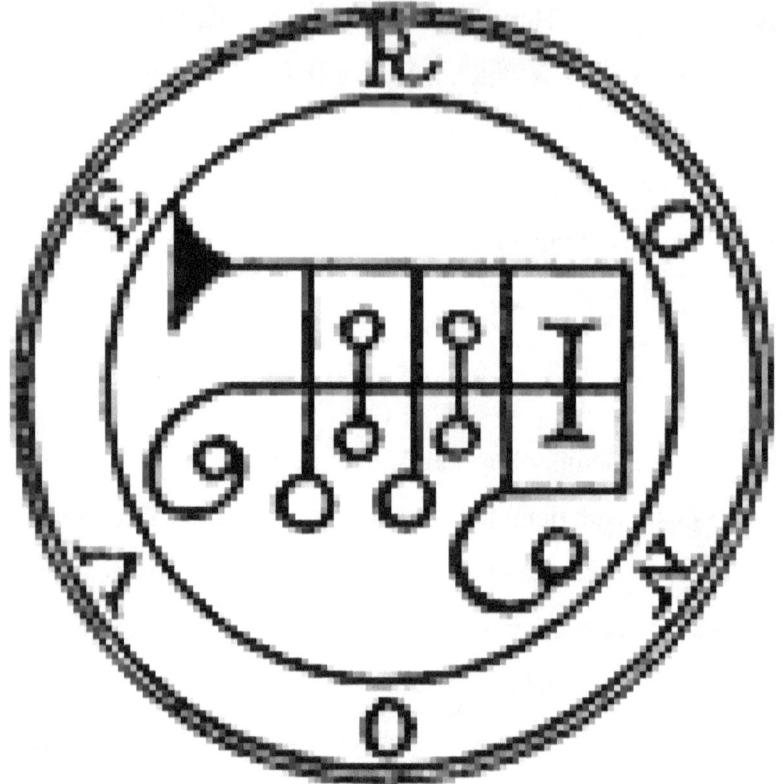

Seal of Renove, aka Ronove

Ri-Chan:

(Mixed Demonology) This demon, has his base in a wide variety of sources, most notably in the realms of Japanese Demonology and surprisingly to some degree in the modern use of interstellar demonology. Online there is a verse in which a person describes conjuring Ri-chan, only to have Ri-chan molest herself and her cousin. However the writer of this account is unwilling to come forward or is unable due to the fact the story has been posted and reposted countless times. Nevertheless, he is described in a physical form as a large 8 foot tale male human, black in color, (the reports say black as in the color black, not to be mistaken with African Americans.) red eyes, large hands and his armor, though made up of what appears to be black, hard scales is actually elastic and moves such as skin. There are accounts of Ri-chan to go from way back as far as the 11th century and most recently two known accounts in 2010 as well as loads of others throughout time.

Rimmon:(Slavic Demonology) This demon is known as Hell's ambassador to the Romanian, Wallachia and Transylvanian region. When ambassadors are in place, it is said no matter what sin a human has done, they would be refused into Hell if the ambassador to a region does not negotiate the capture of the soul and transference of it to the Kingdom of Hell. Which has answered certain things about the afterlife, why some souls are cast into purgatory instead of being forced into Hell or even Heaven (Yes the "Heavens" has ambassadors as well.) Rimmon is known as a ruthless ambassador as he will tax family members in order to achieve goals. He will take a loved one and show them through purgatory and the tortures there for a soul, then when they forfeit whatever Rimmon wants, he will send the soul of the dead to Hell, which is post humorously funny, because he only states to the living, "Would you like to see the soul of your loved one removed from purgatory?" and never states that they would be going to Hell.

Ronobe:(Christian Demonology) A demon that is noted for causing people to "slip up" when speaking to someone about a sensitive subject, and leak information to someone in which the information may devastate, or severely hurt that person. (I.E. Geez Larry, I haven't seen her all night except when she was talking to her ex-boyfriend, and judging by how they were smiling, the ex, might be the new one! Why did you need to speak to her? I'll help you find her if you want me to.) He is described in both demon form as a large aquatic like features such as a sharks head, and human form to resemble a blond haired version of Humphrey Bogart. Note however he does have his demonic talisman symbol tattooed on his left inner wrist and the symbol for a wolf pack on his right inner wrist.

Ronove:(Christian Demonology) He is a Marquis of Hell, he commands 19 legions, teaches languages of the Magicks to humans. He has been known to not be fond of humans who cry and likes to see rage. He is described in the manner of dark hair, and light eyes, with a fondness of hanging out in clubs and bars. One of the few demons that can walk upon "holy ground" of a Christian church due to a pact that was made with Jesus when Jesus was alive.

Ronwe: (Christian Demonology) He was once known as demon of knowledge to the early Christians, and is kno0wn to be a source of lust in men toward sex and greed. He was said to be in charge of 17 legions, however some profess that he is control of 19, and most recently they said he lost control of any legions during the second world war, in which he was spotted in Germany, and through actions that were not his best of all ideas accidently enabled the falling of Berlin.

Roq: (Slavic Demonology) Known for her wickedness, she is known from early gypsy folklore of being able to entice anyone under her will. She in human form is described as rather attractive, red hair and piercing green eyes. She has been spotted by an orthodox priest as recently as 2009 and is known to have a fondness to prey upon older men for the wealth.

Rosier: (Mixed Demonology) His past dates into Egyptian times, and some have considered him to have even an earlier Sumerian roots. He is known for being able to corrupt politicians into full filling his will, and his will alone as he has been banished from the underworld by Satan. The reports have shown that he once tried to steal a wife of

Satan and was never forgiven. He has been known to enable the god Allah to possess the mind of humans, and was once considered a cohort of Muhammad.

Ryaesyn: (Egyptian Demonology) Though the exact origins of Ryaesyn are unknown, there have been traces to Egyptian times as the demon who once tricked Anubis into not allowing the dead to actually die, (which does coincide with the accounts of "Zombies" in the Egyptian region during 3894BC.) Thus, This demon is commonly referred to as a troublemaker in whatever religion Ryaesyn is present. It is known that under Jehovah's beginning reign when the "kingdom of heaven" was based off of a royal court system that man attempted to achieve, Ryaesyn was tempted into service for Jehovah as a court Jester. However it is known Ryaesyn finally took a male form and attempted to fulfill a bestiality act with a dog upon Jehovah's son return from the mortal world. Though this act was in male form, it is said, once Ryaesyn was cast from the Heavens, he became a she, and later an "it" as it is now known that Ryaesyn likes to cause a doubling of sex organs in humans (Hence female born with a testicle or penis, and a male born with ovaries and or vagina.)

S

Sabazios: (Celtic Demonology) The snake, that defended the city of Troy, his followers are commonly referred to as serpent worship. She is described as being as 130 yards, with the maw large enough to swallow a automobile whole. She was recently sighted in South America as a village/cult was discovered to be under his influence as of 2003. There have been unconfirmed sightings in the deserts of Utah as of 2008, however it is not confirmed as the owners of the camcorder were not found, but the video evidence does suggest that there is a cult there worshiping Sabrizios, and apparently conjured Her to eat the owners of the video evidence.

Sabnack: (Mixed Demonology) Also known as Sabnock, this

demon is attached to death programming. If a slave does the "unpardonable sin" against Lucifer and his programming then Sabnack helps insure that the heart of the victim will stop., He is known to appear in the form of an armed soldier, having a lion's head, and riding on a pale-colored horse. It is known he is fond of Swamps, and surprisingly large cities (Only because of the reports in 1997 and 2006, do we assume it is because he is prone to roam sewers during the day.) It is known he has a taste for the human drink Gin, and is said to drink it constantly.

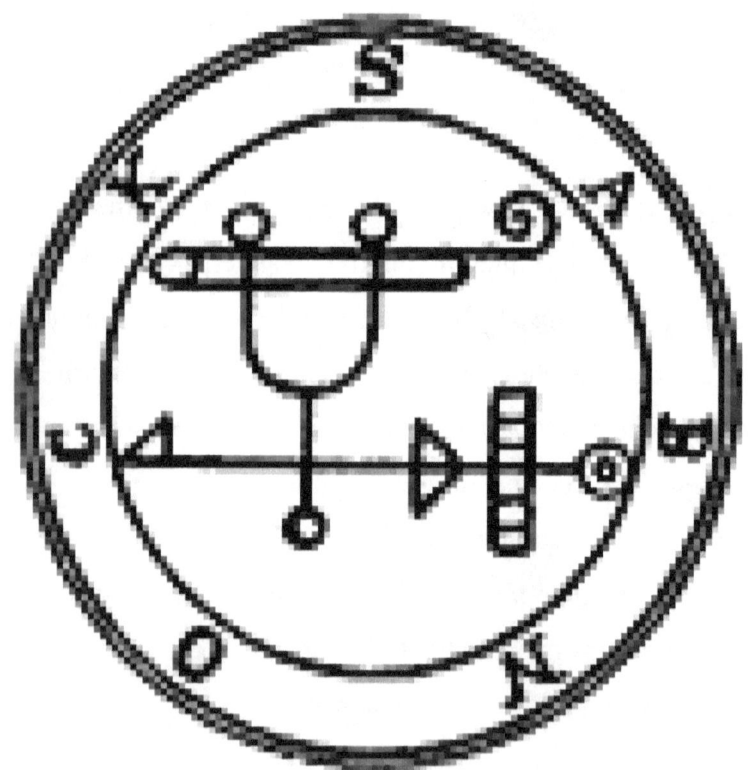

Sadodgenies: (Sumerian Demonology) Demon protector, called upon to protect the perimeter around the covenant or temple of worship. He is one of the few demonic forces to which does not hold a covenant toward one known religion or more. He is known to appear for those who can properly conjure him, which is of course a double surprise, because normally someone who conjures spirit must follow the mythos behind their creation, however in Sadodgenies's case, there is no known mythos that applies. There have been reports as late as 2008 in which he was successfully conjured by using a mixture of Kabbalah and Greek mythos conjuring spells, with a Christian tone added. Sadodgenies is well known to be considered good by those who summon him for their protection, and is said to be one of the demons who even aided Jesus in the 17th year of his life when he was attacked by the negative forces.

Sag: (Nordic Demonology) She is the Daughter of Odin; she is the Goddess of Poetry. Once Jehovah took over the Pantheons, she is known to have once been a celestial wife of Allah. She however had a falling out when she was discovered to have been giving human women the power of strength in fleeing and disobeying their husbands, and Allah was able to banish her to the underworld. In recent years she has been seen in Canada, not far from Alaska. Those who have interacted with her are said to see that she is known to reward men well, providing they show respect and equality towards women.

Sahax:(Mixed Demonology) Sahax is one of the oldest known demons. Her name literally translates into "Old One" and is known as "Forbidden Leader". Legend of the passing of religious pantheons is, Sahax was once the true leader who opposed all positive. It is said that Sahax was the one who suggested to Lucifer that he should overthrow Jehovah, when Jehovah took reign over the main pantheon. He is able to appear on Earth as witnessed as recent as 2009. However, she is only able to be conjured by using the right "summoning spell", and only not surprisingly by a female Aries.

Sakarabru:(African Tribal Demonology) Mostly known to the tribes that have originated in the country of Kenya, Sakarabru, is known as the demon or "dark soul" who waits for human, captures the human and then tortures the human through showing what the "dark things" that human has done it his or her life. It is known that the demon can and will travel as documented in Hawaii in 2005.

Saleos: (Christian Demonology) A great duke in Hell who appears to man as a human soldier, riding on a crocodile, over the centuries he has been known to promote love between the sexes in a way that even the same sex is acceptable in embrace from the very same sex. Little is known about his personal life other than he has been known to have love tryst with human men, and even some human women resulting in the birth of half demon/half humans. (It is said the offspring usually has dark brown eyes by their father and a fondness of the spice oregano)

Samael: (Kabbalah Demonology) Also known as Sammael, Samiel, Simoon and "The Prince of Air". It is thought this angel of death was the demon who tempted Eve. Some scholars have deducted that his name is merely another name for Satan. (Which when you review the case of David Berkowitz aka "The .44 Caliber Killer" and aka "The Son of Sam", most dismiss his visions of his dog speaking to him, and his dog stating that his name was "Sam" as well. This is Ironic because Berkowitz was Jewish and for the Jews, Sammael is the prince of demons. However of course most of those in the world dismiss the paranormal on repeated basis, as stating that it has no tangible proof, and that the actions carried out of a "psychotic nut job" are to be dismiss as hallucinations and or delusions. However, in most cases the age old expression of "If there is smoke, there is some fire" can be applied. Now if truth, I do not believe that Berkowitz was a Satanist. But there is questionable evidence as to if he suffered from a poor mental state or if he was being put in contact with the supernatural. I would suggest the reader please review his case, and take your own investigation. One thing that is interesting is that there was in fact no dog. His neighbor's dog had in fact been dead for over one year before this dog had "suggested" to Berkowitz to commit any murderous acts.) In Rabbinical legend he is a storm demon, and his name is linked with Samiel or Simoon. It is suggested by religious scholars that under the guise of the serpent, tempted Eve in paradise. According to chapters 13 and 14 of the book of Ezekiel (Rabbi Eliezer), Satan's fall was mainly out of jealousy and envy on the part of the angels. The early angels under Jehovah's rein were in fact very jealous of Humans or Man-kind. They were jealous as Man-kind was permitted to name the very things that were on the planet. They saw this act as proving that man was superior to themselves.

Samnu: (Asian Demonology) One of the very few demons from any of the Asian demonology that is able to cross powers over to another realm of thought and in turn can be just as dangerous to come up against as if you were of Christian and or Kabbalah. Some historians have pointed out that that the name and even the demons characteristics have been known for longer than just in the Asian realm of mythology. However most attacks in the past 1,500 years have transpired in Asian lands. (Within the exception in San Francisco in 1998) The demon is known to take on a human form, with striking green eyes, and normal Asian appearance as a male.

Sante-Buisson:(Mixed Demonology) See Verdelet

Sargatanas:(Kabbalah Demonology) A demon, under the command of Forau, He/ She (IT) has a special power of shape shifting in any known size of any known or even unknown object. It is said to produce offspring that live for 38 days, during that time the offspring are well known at hurting humans.

Satan:(Mixed Demonology) In Hebrew the name is Satan, In Arabic, it is Saitan or Shaitan he has been known as the Devil, in later Hebrew and in Christian belief, the supreme spirit of evil, who for immeasurable time has ruled over a kingdom of evil spirits and is in constant opposition to God (Jehovah, later Allah) However his roots run deeper than most think. During the time of the first holy war between Jehovah and Luicifer, The ruler of the underworld was in fact still in control of Hades. Only after Lucifer was confronted by Jehovah and transformed into Lucibel, Hades had agreed to Jehovah to consider turning the underworld pantheon over to "a worthy subject, capable of striking fear into the heart of man." But only if and when Hades would retire, and only if Hades could control the being as well. Now of course Jehovah had bigger issues to deal with such as the coming war with Allah, so when Lucibel had conducted his last and final raid on the main palace in the central part of what most Hebrews and Christians refer to as Heaven, Jehovah finally signed off on the deal to transform Lucibel into Satan. During his time he has been called Diablous in basic Latin, and later Diabolos in Greek. However his true name was closer to Shaitanis, and actually means "The second with sin" as Jehovah felt this was more of an insult to Lucifer/Lucibel, as he was not only being cast into the role as lord of the underworld, but he too would have to serve the older pantheons. There have been known wars between Satan and even his keeper Hades. There was of course the situation in the century leading up to the birth of the Christian Messiah that Satan had tried to gorge Hades with the Sword of Tritactius (Try-tact-tee-us) and of course steal his power through the ritual, but it was thwarted by Zeus, as though Zeus and Hades truly never saw eyes to eyes after Zeus tricked Hades into being lord of the underworld, Zeus still loves his Brother. (There are those who believe this is where the Mormon story of Jesus and Satan being brothers is linked) however, that has never stopped Satan from trying to become the main lord of the underworld. It is known he is permitted to visit his family in heaven every 3 years, and that he does so as for what is equal to 1 day he no longer has to be subject to Hades, but is in fact treated much like he was when he was Lucifer. And it is even said for that one day, even Jehovah throws a very lush banquet in Lucifer's honor. Some attribute this to the 3 year cycle of uprising demonic possessions and incidents that happen during this time period, as Satan takes his "Vacation" the Demons are instructed to keep the humans in terror.

Satanael:(Slavic Demonology) Is a demon of the typical "gargoyle look" Believed to be the evil first son of the God Jehovah by the Bogomil faith. Is known to be seen by humans and will attack if the human provokes him, via getting in the way of him completing his goal. Is known to actually be nice however to humans, but usually for alternative goals, (i.e. will help a human just to hurt 2 or more if possible.)

Sargatanas:(Christian Demonology) He is a major general in the army of Hell. He is known for his cunning tactics and was once known as a possible candidate for transformation and forgiveness by Jehovah. He is said to be the planner when multiple possessions are taking place on the planet, in order to spread the attack out to weaken the churches forces by keeping them stretched out away from each other.

Sarkany:(Mixed Demonology) Was as born the daughter of the famous witch Boszorkany, and is known to have special powers to enable her invisible able to foresee the future while gazing into moving water. Was once a friend with the son of the deity Jehovah, Jesus. Known to still be on the "friends list" and will use her powers for both good and or evil. Was known to have been so fond of Jesus that she attempted to stop his crucifixion, by trying to control Pontius Pilate's mind, until it is said Jesus who noticed her through her cloak of invisibility asked her to stop and allow it to be done. It is said that Sarkany did so out of respect and is known to concentrate herself in the Slavic regions of the planet.

Scox:(Christian Demonology) A Duke of Hell, the main part of known knowledge is that he is a constant liar and thief and is well versed at causing Humans to grow insane. He is described as having the body of a human however the characteristics of an eagle. Last seen in 1911, Nova Scotia.

Sedit: (Kabbalah Demonology) Once known as the Angel Moroni, when he had a passionate battle with the God Allah during the 4th Holy War in the pantheons, Allah employed all the witches he could to curse Moroni into betraying Jehovah. Moroni could not handle the torture, He loved Jehovah so much and yet during this period he felt as if he should try to overthrow and kill Jehovah. So fearing the curse would eventually win, Moroni made his pact with Hades to remove the Evil, so Hades did. However instead of absorbing the evil, Hades left it lay in the swamp and the resulting evil was so strong; it formed into another energy life-force and Sedit was born. He is known to strike against mostly Mormons (After all it was the Angel Moroni is the angel who appeared to Joseph Smith and begat the Mormon movement.) and is even said to revel in the fact when he can cause a Mormon to go against his belief.

Seera: (Mixed Demonology) Also known as Seere in Kabbalah Demonology, this demon is in charge of internal perceptions of time. He can make time fly at whirlwind speed or to slow down. (He is known to appear to most in the form of a beautiful man on a strong winged horse. He brings all things to pass suddenly, transports to any place in the twinkling of an eye, and discovers all thefts. Most humans if not all can summon him, and it is known that great joy or great fear will usually attract him to a situation. He is indifferently good or bad, and will do the will of the operator. He is known to have sat on the minister councils in both Central hell and Eastern Heaven, under Jehovah's reigns. He is well versed in diplomacy, and is well known as a tormenter of thieves, so much to the fact he is known to slow down incarceration time for thieves as a double punishment for stealing. Most hard-core Christians deem him evil because they are unaware of the neutral or even good demons. However, in retrospect these are the very same people who get tormented by evil angels. Most who pray or "summon" Seera with good intentions benefit from it. However avoid him if theft is in your heart.

Sekhmet: (Egyptian Demonology) Once known as the an Egyptian deity of war, this lioness goddess eventually became the demon of Vengeance one Zeus came to power. She is known to be shown in human form as recent as 1998. She loves to take the side of a jilted lover and is known to "suggest" to a jilted lover that the object of their desire should "not go on without them." The only to combat said demon is to line your home with a mixture of salt and dried lemon peel, ground to a powder and placed on your property. You can do so in the name of another deity, just make sure you never call out her name while doing it, as shown in the past it doesn't fight against her, it is like "ringing the dinner bell" for your relationship.

Semiazas: (Christian Demonology) Known to be the chief of all fallen angels after Satan came to power. Even to this day, Angels from time to time step out of grace with the main deity in charge, Jehovah. When they do they are sent of course to the care of Semiazas, who reviews them and sees if a negotiation can be worked out with Jehovah for "taking them in" or "discharging them back to Jehovah's care or even "back to Earth". It is known that Semiazas is a good negotiator as there are still many darker demons locked up in the prisons in Western heaven.

Separ:(Kabbalah Demonology) Quite possibly the most famous Incubus known, he is a great duke, who appears in red apparel and armed like a soldier, He is well known for drawing women into a state of strong sexual desire for their lovers, and then re-shaping himself to appear in their lovers form, then of course taking advantage of it. He is well known and active, his most recent attacks have taken place in 2007 in Detroit, Michigan, and oddly enough a case in Florida in 2008, 2009, and 2010. The Florida case is unique in that for the very first reported times, and interviews with the examining exorcist, Separ did not take form. It was confirmed that it was Separ by the attending priests. However, it is believed that the case in Michigan weakened him, as it involved four separate ministers.

Seraphim:(Christian Demonology) One of the few demons who can easily transverse the bridge between "Heaven and Hell" and is well known to be both good at times and evil at times. Now much can be said about her as she is typically seen with bluish gray skin and piercing blue eyes. She is known to hang out in New Orleans, Louisiana and or any larger city with a decent amount of "Magick practices" and or "Gothic sub-culture". Was known as recently as 2010 to take on various human "Lovers" that happen to be overweight or obese, both male and or female and It is said she absorbs their fat cells during sleep in effort to keep her healthy. Which often can only be compared to as a "Psychic Vampire" attack, only instead of Energy being drawn, the obese person looses weight. There have been no drastic reports, and she is known to only take a lover for no more than 4 months.

Sereca: (Kabbalah Demonology) Her profession is that of a "Secret" demon. Known to possess humans from time to time (The last recorded one was in 2009) she has a tendency to possess children. She especially likes to possess children who are heavy into their chosen religion, and will stop at nothing to get her true goal and that is to sway the faith of an adult in the mix of those who attempt to deal and or exorcise her from the child. Some believe her chosen targets is because she was once human and that she indeed was apart of a family that tore itself up once Christ made his presence known to man here on Earth. The reason why her profession is "secret" is because those who have been in contact with her, have a tendency to forget what the conversation was about, only to have it remain a "secret" until later on in the humans life, there is a trigger event that will remind them of the conversation. Some attribute her "secret attacks" as to the reason why some people experience déjà-vu, in which she has given a memory to someone of their future, and they experience it later.

Sese: (Christian Demonology) known as the Demon of War and Strife, he will stop at nothing to gain a fight of some sort between humans he comes into contact with. If seen he is considered to be a good looking male, dressed in better clothing and usually with blonde hair and blue eyes. His skin is described to look almost matching to a human who has had constant tanning bed processes. (It is described a very orange tan like appearance.) There is a confirmation of him speaking to both George W. Bush and Saddam Hussein, however the reports have to be faulty as the person described was seen with each other in virtually the very same hour of September 23rd, 2001.)

Set: (Mixed Demonology) Also known as Seth, and or Osiris, He is one of the few demons who still possess full blown deity powers. Once other deities ruled the main pantheon, Set became a demon of his own choice under the Kabbalah, Judeo and Christian faiths. He is known to not only torment other gods, but will even torment Satan himself (which Set was once in charge of the underworld, before Hades assumed the role.) Set will not fall in any battle, his power rivals that of other deities who have a large worship from humans, and will actually grow stronger if a human disbelieves in him, after all he still a deity. He is known to torment those who worship him in their desire. If they attempt to gain notoriety and power through the use of him or his power, he will strike when the least expect at them. He loves to absorb a humans financial situation and has been known to cause most if not all of those who worship him to lose financial stability and in the end go broke. However he does have a "soft side" he hates it when humans abuse animals and children and has known to come to their aid if needed.

Shaba-lidoma:(Mixed Demonology) This demon has one, true ability when it comes to tormenting humans, and that is the case of depression. He is known to cause depression to the point of suicide in humans, and now comes the odd part, it is said that he died of suicide himself. Some reported cases in the past have been of various people who possess money, love and stability in their lives to all of a sudden commit the act of suicide. Most cases have shown his symbol somewhere nearby the suicide. Ironically every time the symbol is saved for investigation, it has been destroyed or lost. In 2002 a priest attempted to snap a photo of the symbol painted on the wall in the blood of a victim who painted the symbol on the wall near his suicide by slitting his wrist, and painting it in his blood. The report is the camera died shortly afterwards and all pictures were lost as the camera had the film removed for development. The symbol is described as a 9 point star, with an indescribable symbol in the center involving a triangle and 4 lines (one out of each side and two at the bottom) protruding outward. Wish a series of lines and squiggles in the center.

Shabriri:(Kabbalah Demonology) A demon that is well known for striking upon the blind, and a description is not available other than in her presence is always the odor of what has been described as rotting bread and cabbage.

Shax:(Christian Demonology) Known for his abilities to fool Exorcist and achieve full blown possession after a trial exorcism. One of the few demons that can handle direct sunlight, and is known to even be able to enter a church and even take place in the symbolic ritual of communion as standard Christian forces do not have any ability upon him. It is known during the crucifixion of Christ, he was disguised as a Roman soldier and it is suggested that he is the one who supposedly held out a chalice and drank the direct blood of Christ. No matter the holy ground in question, it is known he can cross the threshold with little to no issues. *(See seal symbol on next page)*

Seal of Shax

Shemhazai: (Mixed Demonology) He is classed as an Arch/Fallen in Christian lore, as he was along Lucifer during the initial war with Jehovah. He somehow survived the mission he was in charge of by attacking the sacred library in the Central Heaven Pantheon. He led an assault of 33 other angels who was sent to slaughter and destroys the library and its inhabitants. Needless to say, they managed their task by literally blowing it up. This infuriated Jehovah so much as his written family history was stored there as well as the ancient texts of Tlepish. Which of course was the actual texts that enable deities to achieve any and all powers, so by it being lost, Jehovah decided to remain in power without retiring, because no other god would be able to keep control and humanity in a constant state of war and peace to enable the world to go one growing and changing. (Which is even more funny as the text is stored in other pantheons, however Jehovah would have to surrender his duty to the ruler of those pantheons, and it is not a case of not wanting to retire as it is, they refuse to come out of retirement, though there have been well known statements from Ra.)

Shilo:(Christian Demonology) The Destructor, the wicked, the unworthy, Shilo is known as one of the most incredible sources for evil. However now comes the real odd part. Shilo did not exist until the 16th century. Some believe that it had to have been the most wicked person alive, and almost became a saint only instead of serving God, Shilo serves evil, nothing but evil. Even though Shilo has only presented itself (I should say "herself" as Shilo has a tendency to take female form) at last known reports 219 times. Each time, there is nothing more than pain and suffering for humans. The only known defense is, a version of holy water (Or moonbeam water if Pagan) and oddly enough vinegar, sugar and tomato (yes, ketchup will work). Mix together and throw it in the direction of Shilo.

Shiq: (Christian Demonology) A demon known for taunting those who are traveling, and seriously it doesn't matter where you traveling, If you are on a trip and you see a serious accident or have been involved in an accident, there is a good chance that Shiq has had a hand in it. Some say it is because Shiq was an angel who was assigned to earth and when the angels had the uprising against Jehovah, shiq was headed to heaven for his years of perfect duty to Jehovah, but as Lucbel had came from Lucifer, and was finally being set into existence as Satan, he was being cast into the underworld that would eventually be referred to as Hell. As Shiq was arriving Satan and the other ex-angels were being cast out, and Jehevah accidently cast Shiq into the group, thus Shiq swore anger against Jehovah for his mistake, and now serves Satan.

Shiva: (Hindu Demonology) Once a powerful Goddess who now serves the powers of darkness under the dark pantheons. When Jehovah came to power, she swore her love for Lucifer as she was overcome with his beauty. Later when Lucifer decided to overthrow

Jehovah, she fought on his side from the outer Pantheons.

Shony: (Slavic Demonology) This water demon is well known in the regions of the North Sea, even though he is listed under the doctrine of Slavic demonology, he is well known to the sailors who sail upon the North Sea. He will sink any vessel if he deems to do so. Some have claimed that he was involved in the destruction of many oil platforms, and has been described as being seen their as well. He is known to have 3 hydra-snake like heads and is typically black and dark green in color. It is known that he cannot stand to be out of water long, so he will usually attack during a rainstorm. He is known to have made his way on land twice, once in 1678 and again in 1993. There are still sacrifices made to him yearly to this day. In most cases it is a crew that is under stack who takes a newer crew member and slits his throat then dumping him overboard. The Viking shipbuilders are well known to take logs, and then tie a victim to the log, then plunging it thirty miles off of the coast. In modern times, Shoney is well known and is appeased regularly.

Shub: (Mixed demonology) This demon has many origins, however like in most cases of mixed origins, the demon is easily described as a translation from one culture to the next. It is known that anything positive works against Shub, such as Holy Water, Positive Magick and so forth, and in Shub's appearance in 1998, even an Atheist can evoke a positive power over Shub. Shub is known to love areas with warmer weather, and lots of water. Maybe that could explain that his last 6 sightings have been near Florida and Louisiana, Is known that he will take on the appearance of a well to do Human male, only obvious goal is to cause destruction whenever possible. He has been known for loving it when a family is destroyed, and will try to negotiate any deal where it will bring things to a very bad outcome.

Shui-Mu:(Chinese Demonology) – Though she is known as a Chinese water demon, Shui-Mu is well known to attack most bodies of water. Ironically it is said that she must return to Taihu Lake, a large lake in the Yangtze Delta plain, on the border of the Jiangsu and Zhejiang provinces in the People's Republic of China every 6 years. In the mean time she can even assume human form and attack humans. She is well known to seduce men and kill them. Usually the victim is found with his lungs filled with water, and all of the salt in his body was virtually doubled in his body. One of the biggest situations took place in 1918, in which she was returning to her home, the local holy men, has set a trap for her. They set a young child in a large bowl, when she crept up to it she transformed herself into her normal appearance from human form, opened her mouth and began to eat the child. But the child was in fact a decoy and was not real. The decoy was filled with herbs, salt and the chain was in fact silver. She bit down and was in shock, she couldn't move. The chain's end, protruding from her mouth, welded itself chains remaining in the dish. Bound and powerless, the demon was led away to be fastened securely at the bottom of a deep well, where she was to remain a prisoner for all times. However in June 1978, it was known during that the cult that worshipped her, managed to get her released in the middle of the night. The people of that province say that the end of the chain can be seen whenever the water level in the well drops particularly low. We know she was in fact most recently in Ohio, 2011.

Silcharde: (Christian Demonology) One of the demons who may be summoned by necromancy, known for his ability to insure the person who summoned him is granted wishes in almost a Ginn fashion, however it can be a random amount of wishes, Silcharde will stop at nothing to insure the wisher experiences "Hell on Earth."

Sitri:(Mixed Demonology) This spirit is well known as the seducer of anyone who seeks a "sexual release" well known to cause someone to appear more physically attractive, in order to get the subject into a passionate sexual situation, so passionate in fact that the couple (Or more in some situations) will develop emotions for the other parties affection, and just as the other party is giving into the emotional side of a commitment, Sitri will undo the physical attractiveness, and cause emotions on the subject to be crush (To the point of suicide in most cases.)

Smoyax: (American Southern Baptist Demonology) Though some have claimed that this demon does in fact have a base in earlier versions through African Voodoo, there is no actual recorded situation involving Smoyax until 1876 in Alabama in which the demon was fought off by ex-slaves who were practicing a mixture of African Magick and Baptist rights. The demon is reported to have slaughtered 39 men, women and children. Also was reported that the demon also killed over 100 animals of livestock. The demon was seen as recent in the swamps of Louisiana, in 1995.

Solxs: (Kabbalah Demonology) She is well known by those who follow the works of Crowley. She was documented to have been one of the demons that he had conjured in his life. It was known that when he spent three months at his home by Loch Ness (Yes remember some referred to as "the other Loch Ness Monster") it was spent conjuring and conversing with Solx. When she is present near humans, she is known to make humans "unleash" their inhibitions.

Sonnilion: (Slavic Demonology) Once considered the "Angel of Hate", she was later purported as a demon, as she led the attacks on Muslim Turks who invaded Romania in 1402, which they proceeded to rape and murder her half human daughter, Ware. After that, Sonnilion went into flat out rage and has been known to slaughter Muslims on sight. She has no love for Jehovah, but it is her hatred of any of the followers of Allah that was the enabling factor to have her daughter join her on Earth after her death.

Stolas: (Christian Demonology) He is well known as a Grand Prince of Hell. He commands twenty-six legions. He normally appears in the shape of an owl, however he is known that when he appears before exorcists, he will assume the shape of a male man. He is known to be able to trick most exorcists into committing suicide, as he will reflect on the exorcist life and play it against him. *(See seal symbol on next page)*

Seal of Stolas

Succorbenoth: (Christian Demonology) Known to protect the main waterway leading from the River Styx into Hell/Underworld, if you are caught trying to escape from hell through his passage, he will turn men into eunuchs and close castrate women as well. It is said he resembles a Hydra with four arms, dark purple/black in color.

Surgat: (Kabbalah Demonology) A demon who may be summoned only on the 3rd and 9th full moons of any solar year, and once summoned, Surgat will give magick abilities to the person who summoned them for the remainder of the moon, until it goes dark. However, there is a cost. Until the new moon grows into a full one, the person who summoned will lose life-force, and has been known to even cause some to grow old to death, so the first thing to do is swell your life-force to full, and even some de-aging spells would be in order, as the magick power given is known to not be affected once the new moon has arrived.

Sytry: (Mixed Demonology) This demon, automatically attaches itself to any altar that any woman who has shown her naked body too for financial gain. Commonly and even jokingly called the "Patron Saint of Strippers" Sytry has been known to affect any female he deems fit to conform to removing her clothing in presence of a male.

T

TA:(Mixed Demonology) TA is well known as a apprehender demon, he will hunt you down wherever you are at. He began his line of work during the Sumerian days, follow through working for the Egyptians and eventually ended up working for Hades and Satan. There have been countless reports of him over the centuries, and each time the only description that has been offered seems to fit the description of the "Predator Alien" from the films "Predator" and "Aliens vs. Predator". Green and yellow reptilian skin, hard leathery dreadlock type hair, and a gaping maw for a mouth seem to pretty much fit the mold. (Remember the old expression, that "art imitates life.")

Tando Ashanti:(Asian Demonology) Was once a god, now under the outcomes of the last 3 Holy Wars, he has been cast in demonhood, he is known as the one who demands the simultaneous human sacrifice of seven men and seven women, to which he will offer god like power to the sacrifices for no less, but no more than 18 years. However none of the sacrifices must be without virginity, or he deducts 1 year off. Some hear of this and say, "Wow 17 years as a god" and then they have to be reminded that they are in need of 5 others to make the bargain.

T'an-mo:(Asian Demonology) Know in most Asian Demonology (though mainly Chinese) as the demon of desire. He is known to conjure lust for almost anything in the most docile of humans. Has been known to have a fondness of citrus fruit and an even greater fondness of causing desires in people of power that will cause a great loss of "underlings" lives.

Tat:(Egyptian Demonology) Once considered a great human who was almost a Demi-god, Tat began her career as a demon in a most peculiar way, she was known to have helped Moses rescue his people. Now before you say, "What? Huh? Why?" allow me to explain, she helped Moses, and in turn after he had brought his people to the land of their own, she showed up thinking that Moses would embrace her, However due to the fact she possessed great power, Moses ordered her to stay away in the "name of Jehovah", hence she began her activities which no doubt gained her to the demon-hood under Satan himself.

Tcalyel:(Native American Demonology) Once a female spirit known for her power over things in the night time, she went on to become a demon under the reign of power inflicted during the early Holy Wars. The exact reason for her turning into a demon is not completely unknown, however it does have its chance surrounding mystery. All that is known is she somehow stepped into favor with dark forces as she was the sufferer of a broken heart. Many have speculated who it was who had broken her heart, some have even speculated it was Jehovah or even the Angel Mormoni.

Tchort: (Slavic Demonology) Often referred to as the "Black God" he is well known by most on the Eastern Block of Europe. He has a great power, and an equally great distaste for Jehovah. Some have mistaken him for Satan, however we know this to be false as Tchort possess the power to walk upon Holy ground and even has been known to walk into a Christian Church (And in 1998 completely level one.) man of those who are wishing to become a Vampire or other dark creature has been known to summon him in hopes to achieve this goal.

Tezcatlipoca: (Aztec Demonology) This demon is well known to be conjured by using a mirror or a water reflection when you summon him. He is well known for the realm of destruction he will bring with him. Even though he is of Demonic Blood, he is known to be able to go into the Pantheons of Light with ease. Some believe this actually credits him as an Arch-Demon as he has the ability to do so, however some are quick to point out that he can only be summoned using a Zinc based talisman, hence dark Magick.

Tezrian: (Christian Demonology) Known for her sexual escapades in seducing women, she also is known for her lust of War. She is known to appear almost in the form of female of South American base (dark hair, dark eyes) and is even known to speak in a somewhat Brazilian accent. She is very well known to desire women who are normal considered "straight" and be in a relationship with a "man of power" that in turn because she controls the female of the relationship, she controls the man as well through suggestions.

Thamuz: (Sumerian Demonology) He is an ambassador of Hell. Well known to have excellent negotiation skills and was reported to have infiltrated the Church and was said to have been in council with Torquemada, and in turn is believed to have started the Spanish Inquisition. Later when the Inquisition was done, he popped up again in history only to have invented artillery. It was said that Adolph Hitler had altars built and ceremonies conducted to summon him into the soul of Rommel. However during the end of World War II, the most credible records of these acts were either lost or destroyed. But we do know of the Statue of Thamuz that was built within a summoning circle that was just outside the City of Berlin.

Thiassa: (Nordic Demonology) Was once a Demi-God, and even had a dispute with Thor. Once the Christian Pantheon became the dominant one, and Thor was considered to be an ally by Jehovah, he granted Thor whatever he wished, it is said by the time Thor Spoke, Thiassa was on fire and emerged in demon form from the flames. Because of their fued, some have even speculated that is why the early Nordic versions of the Christian Crosses feature Thor's Hammer as a way of taunting Thiassa.

Thoth: (Egyptian Demonology) Once considered the Egyptian god of Magick, Thoth took his place by Satan's side as a co-hort as Jehovah banned the use of Magick by Humans and was very displeased when Thoth was one of the revolutionaries who believed humans were of no use to the Gods. Many have tried to summon usually fail in regards they use Egyptian based summoning. Thoth can be summoned through a Anti-Christian ceremony with Egyptian overtones as he is well documented to swear allegiance to Satan during the early Holy Wars.

Th'uban: (Muslim Demonology) A demon well known for just wanting to live on the planet but reeking dismay to humans, with a love for destruction and chicken, mostly appears in the shape of a "dragon type" being.

Tiamat: (Christian Demonology) A demon that guards the southernmost gate of Hell, well known for his cruelty to animals and has been known to take form on Earth and seduce younger men.

Tiwaz: (Slavic Demonology) He used to be worshipped by many of the locals in the areas throughout eastern Germany as a god until Christianity came around. We know he used to demand human sacrifices in his name before he fell out of favor with the people. However we do know that at least there are still small cults whom worship him to this day and in all cases there are human disappearances which happen to coincide with the Slavic Witchcraft calendar. The most recent of these disappearances was as recent as 2011. And we do know that his cult has shown up in both England and in America.

Tlacatecolototl: (Native American Demonology) He is the demon of a stormy night. He is well known in the American southwest, and many have reported seeing his Gargoyle type shape attacking livestock on the most rough and perilous nights with lots of thunder and lightning. He is well known to have acquired the taste for beef and bison. He was discovered hiding out amongst a river in Arizona in 1998 and has not been found since.

Troian: (Slavic Demonology) She is well known as the demon whom loves to steal Children and "alter" them into food to serve back to other humans. Some have stated that the fairy tale of Hansel and Gretel was based on upon the knowledge of Troian and her ways of turning children into food to be eaten. Ironically on a side note, she does have a well known taste for gingerbread goods as well. She has red hair and green eyes and was seen last in 2003 (with a disappearance of 9 children.)

Tunrida:

(Christian Demonology) A master demon, she is well known as one of the past wives of Satan, and actually had a love affair with Jehovah just before his rise to power as king of the Pantheons. She is known to have beautiful golden hair and crystal blue eyes. She is also known for being attracted to human men who have a very low self worth, to which she will turn the male into a "new man" and cause him to gain a vanity that is very high, to where he becomes a threat to everyone including himself.

Typhon: (Mixed Demonology) Was once an Egyptian god, however once Jehovah came to rise, Typhon took over as the lord of North hell. There are some reports to which it is said that Satan himself is in fear of Typhon as he has shown tremendous power. Some has stated that Typhon should have been lord of the underworld; however he did not wish for it, and declined the offer. Some cults still worship Typhon to this day, and they are easy to spot as they by trade must be missing their left eye. It has to do with the rituals invited by the demon, if they remove their left eye, then he will enable a "spiritual eye" that will enable them to see.

U

Uaq:(Christian Demonology) Her job is a very interesting on, as she is the demon who is known to tempt "men of god" to commit sin. Some have said that she was spotted in the 1980s hanging around the American evangelical preachers, and was even the one who brought forth the thoughts of desire and lust into the hearts of famous preachers. Uaq especially loves to set the act of "sinning" in the heart of the intended so much, that it is the guilt that brings them into admitting their wrongdoing. She will stop at nothing, albeit sexual desire or just flat out greed. She is known to love it when a focal point of Jehovah or Jesus becomes that in which they speak against.

Uayc:(Christian Demonology) To say either him or her for this demon is a it of a stretch. There has never been a given sexual orientation associated with Uayc. According to the memoirs of St. Benedict, he faced off against this specific demon in the year 548AD. He in fact is the one who founded most of the best ways to fight Uayc. We know by St. Benedict's standoff with Uayc that bronze will subdue the demon, almost paralyzing it. We also know that the bronze theory is true as recognized during a standoff again in 1986 and again in 2009. The demon for the better degree is a "searcher" demon. Its job is to track lost souls who escaped hell, but majorities of encounters with Uayc have turned up the demon is primarily searching for items and or people who a person that summoned Uayc asks for. It is surprising that the basic conjuring spell will call it forth, which normally a demon of this power and agility in tormenting humans requires a bit of a stronger spell for conjuring up. Due to the fact the demon is easily summoned, it is best to keep bronze near, as in the case in 2009, a devote Christian fundamentalist politician has summoned the demon in order to carry out a specific goal.

Ukobach: (Mixed Demonology) He is the main fire engineer of Hell. Used to work for Hades and others throughout the ages, finally works in modern day hell for whoever is in charge. Is known to be given passage to heaven on occasion when their fires need tending to, and likes to spend his "vacations" on earth. Has been known to meet women and cause them to produce offspring which happen to be "firebugs" or arsonist.

Ulle: (Nordic Demonology) Was once the Nordic "God of the Chase, now is the primary leader for the tracking of renegade angels, deity's and the "damned" who attempt to flee into the upper pantheons such as those rules by Ra, Zeus and Jehovah. He has complete access to the upper pantheons and is well known to dislike being sent on a chase for souls on Earth or any other "living realm"

Ullikummi: (Mixed Demonology) Once an ancient Sumerian demon, now known to pander his way through existence by causing harm to humans and others in modern day. Some call him the "Pirates Demon" as he is well known as believer in piracy of anything in any form.

Unsere: (Kabbalah Demonology) She was once a goddess, and in fact was once the wife of Jehovah, however after she was caught aiding mankind with sorcery and Magick, she was shunned by Jehovah. She even had a lurid affair with Lucifer before he came to his power, and some have even suggested that she may have been the reason for Lucifer to renounce Jehovah. It is know that she will take human form and interfere with humans, especially those who seek the help of the church.

Uphir: (Kabbalah Demonology) A demon, who actually heals others in the name of Satan. When many have prayed for a miracle, and offered their soul in exchange, it is Uphir who actually heals the sick and wounded. Has no known sworn allegiances to Satan, some believe that he got the job because he helped Hades from time to time, and even attended to Jesus once. He for the better term is nothing but a doctor who happens to be a demon.

Ura:
(Mixed Demonology) He was once the Babylonian spirit of disease, and once came up with the concept to destroy all of humans and other living creatures on the planet; however he was thwarted by

Ishun, who was once the council to humans via the early gods. Ishun knew the weakness of Ura in Pine. He had all weapons coated in pine resin and even used pine cones as an early form of a "grenade". Even the scent of pine is known to have a paralyzing effect on Ura, and was used in 1969 when Ura attacked a small tribe in South America.

Uvall: (Christian Demonology) He is the Duke of the main gates to hell, commanding 36 legions; He has complete knowledge of the past, and future. Satan himself is a constant employer of his knowledge in regards of how to defeat Jehovah. Most Christians will try to dismiss that fact as they believe Jehovah and his son to be the complete source of power in regards that they believe that Jehovah will win the "Last Holy War" however as any ex-angel, ex-demon or any other previous deity has been interviewed and or questioned, they all have admitted that "no deity can posses the ability to win the final battle until the final battle has been fought." When probing further into the matter, it was uncovered as Jehovah's boasting about winning the final battle was nothing more than propaganda at best, much like any leader does to taunt and frighten the enemy. Uvall has complete knowledge of what is going to happen, and always admits, "every day the outcome changes."

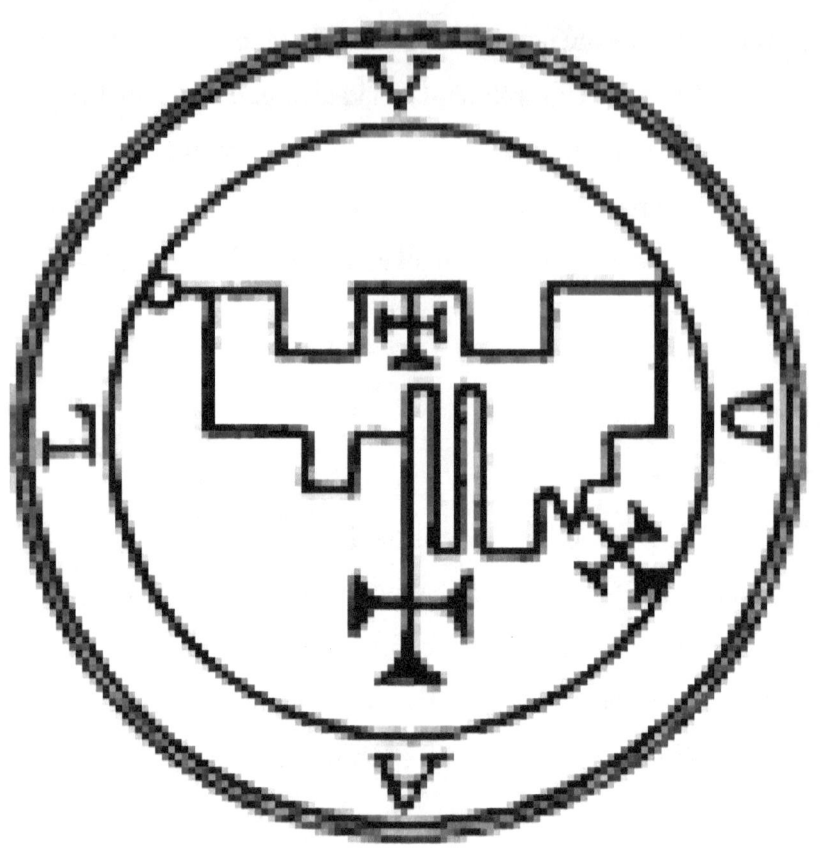

V

Vae: (Christian Demonology) He replaced the former master portal keeper Xamm when Jehovah came to power. And also enforces Jehovah's main rules that only Demons, Angels and Deities should be the ones who transverses of the Master Portals that connect our world with others such as the Spirit realms and Pantheons. However, he is easily fooled and prone to taking Vacations from his position.

Valac: (Kabbalah Demonology) Known by most on the Occult world as the "Great Puppet Master", Valac likes to live amongst the humans and more importantly likes to find way to control them. He is very intense when it comes to making plans, it is almost as if he can plan for chaotic and what can be unconsidered outcomes to make the plan arrive at his final planned outcome. Some have considered his tactics and extensive planning and considered him a master tactician, with one small drawback, he cannot plan a battle at all for some reason, but when it comes to a social setting, he is very ingenious. One of his favorite plans is to have a spouse to cheat on another, and have the other one find out and then murder-suicide become the outcome.

Valafar:(Christian Demonology) He is a grand duke of hell; it is known his section is considered to be the upper east end. He commands 10 legions, and appears in the shape of a lion. He is considered tolerant to the ones who have been banished to hell by sins of Murdering another human, however if you do something smaller like steal or rape, it is said you have to do a lot to earn his trust.

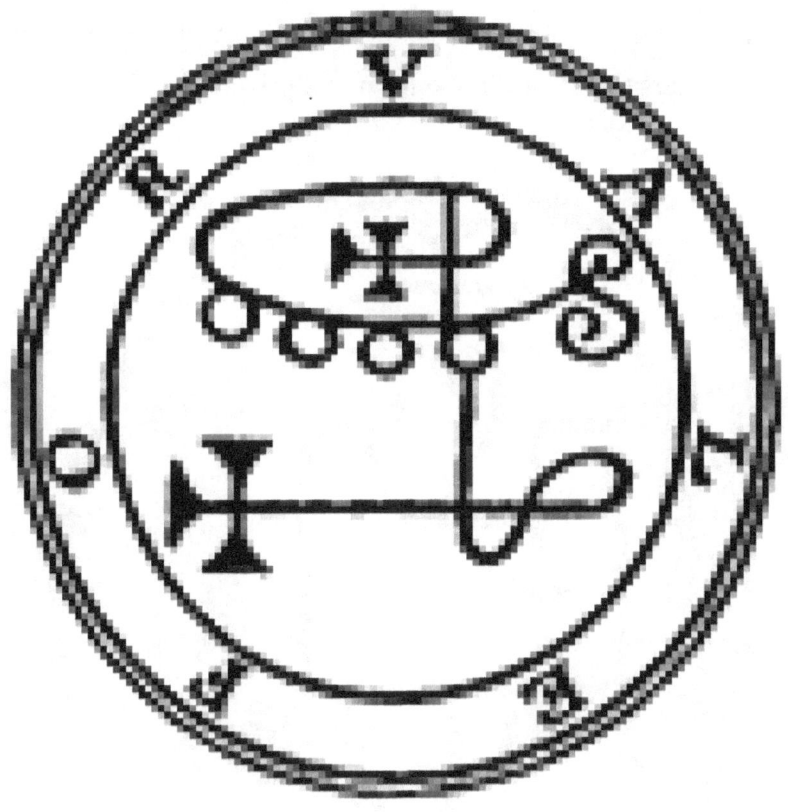

Vanth: (Mixed Demonology) One of the brides of Satan, she loves to taunt teenagers who have died and been sent to hell. She is well known as a demon who infiltrates teen social circles and leads someone to gain their trust, then disposes of them as they carry out her bidding. One of her known favorites is to especially cause incest to happen within a family.

Vapula: (Christian Demonology) A strong duke, He doesn't formally command any legions, but is well versed in military philosophy. He normally appears to humans in the form of a griffin.

Vassago: (Slavic Demonology) Once out the direct care of Hell, Vassago for the better degree can actually be considered 'good". He likes to see children smile and laugh, and has a supreme disregard for Satan after Satan betrayed him during the battle of Argos.

Vara: (Mixed Demonology) Vara for the better part of description, the textbook version of a succubus, She slyly puts herself into a human's life and make the human feel complete love for her, then she leaves and causes much despair. Her often used tactic is that of taking the form of a human's desire, seduce the human then leave the human to suffer and in most cases cause the human to either commit suicide and or murder in the name of love and lust.

Veard: (Kabbalah Demonology) Veard is the one demon who can literally drive humans to the breaking point of destruction. He has appeared many times throughout history, and always in a situation that can leave one wondering why. He is sharp tongued and very quick to witted when it comes to forming a plan that will cause destruction, he has been seen with Dr. Oppenheimer during the Manhattan Project, as one of the "scientist" and even was known to be a confidant of Osama Bin laden during the summer of 1999. No doubt whenever he is involved with a human, there will be an end result of large amounts of death and destruction.

Velak: (Mixed Demonology) This demon is well known for her ability and that is pure shock value to a situation. She will stop at nothing to cause a human the shriek in either disgust or just shock in general; it can be anything from causing a human to be frightened to seeing ones house catch on fire. In the end, her one goal is merely to shock humans. Some have suggested she may have worked for the Fox Network at one time, of course this has never been proven.

Veltis:(Kabbalah Demonology) He was invoked by using the spells of Solomon, and can even be summoned in modern day by using them. An evil spirit who assaulted St. Margaret of Cortona, Italy (died 1297), but was overcome by her. It is known by prior incidents and the most recent sighting in 2011 that he can overcome by Olive Oil.

Vepar:(Mixed Demonology) She will appear as a mermaid, and can be conjured by sorcery only on saltwater, and if the conjuring human is not within sight of land, (so yes must be out on a boat, ship, etc.) and she will do the bidding of the human who summoned her. However she does not appear to those who call her out of the correct season, though she prefers warm tropical waters, she has been known to appear for those who have called her in the most frigid of waters. *(See seal symbols on next page)*

Seal of Vepar for summoning in Winter and Spring

Seal of Vepar for summoning in summer and Autumn

Verdelet: (Christian Demonology - through a mixed background) A demon that is known of her love for witches, she is said to be well known to take human form and seduce male witches, enabling them great power. Once known in formal hell as the Master of Infernal ceremonies, she had a past which is very extensive in Kabbalah, Egyptian and Greek lore's. She is known to be very adept at garnering power over the strongest of believers in other faiths. (Example: If you are devout in your faith, such as Christianity, do not pray from any deity for help. He power is built on reverse energy, the more you pray or summon a deity for protection, the more power she gets. If you were to pray or summon a deity such as Jehovah, you in turn would build her power to the very same level as Jehovah. The only way to defeat her is to provide strength in you and command her directly. She cannot garner strength and is powerless.

Verin: (Christian Demonology) Known for her ability to cause impatience in humans, she loves to torment them through invoking impatience. She is well known as hanging out in retail locations, waiting for a line to form by a checkout counter, and having a human approach the "boiling point" Next time you are in that position, and you are having moments of waiting for a few minutes really get to you, look around and see if you find a woman smiling with content, it may be Verin in human disguise.

Vetis: (Kabbalah Demonology) Well known as the demon of holy corruption, this demon thrives on temptation of those who seek things in the name of god (mainly Jehovah, Jesus or Allah, but not limited to those) Well known to take human form to achieve his goals, and does well at it. Many of the evangelical preachers who have been caught stealing from the churches have been tempted into it by Vetis.

Vine: (Mixed Demonology) In Christian Demonology, he is great king and earl, and normally appears in a monstrous form; however he can take shape of a human if commanded. At command of an exorcist, he will build a tower or a wall to protect the good from evil, and has even been known to be easily commanded to reveal a witch.
(See seal symbol on next page)

Seal of Vine

Vritra: (Hindu Demonology) This "Enemy of the Gods" usually appears as a serpent, in normal Huindu faith, however once she became liberated through the clashes that took place during the early holy wars, she begat the role of a Demon. She is has a special ability as a tempter of one sex to become attracted to another of the same sex, by casting a "haze" over another, to which the intended target finds the other attractive in a way that he normally would be towards the opposite sex. It is not a "homo-demon", it just likes to play this trick. Some say because of the sexual confusion is how she gains power. He last known appearance begat in Oslo, Sweden in August, 2003 to which the there was a massive uproar as she apparently played her trick. It was doubly not well received by the Gay, Lesbian and Transgendered community who had to deal with the rash of pregnancies and births the following year, as she apparently had even cause Gay Men who were normally attracted to men, to find women attracted and the same for Lesbians, who somehow found men attractive as well.

Volarire: (Mixed Demonology) He is one of the famous gate-keepers, Known for his love of games in general. Some speculate because of this desire he has for games that he usually is the gate-keeper for the nearest portal by Las Vegas which is not far from Phoenix, Arizona. However, most reports are that he is actually the Gate-keeper assigned to the Portal by Reservoir Dovois in Canada.

Vual: (Christian Demonology) A great duke, when summoned he will come first as an enormous dromedary, However upon command he will assume human form and speaks in the Egyptian tongue, as his one true birth-right was on the Egyptian Pantheon. He procures the love of women, and then looses interest in them. He has one known goal and that is to see foes join together in a bond of friendship. This is all too funny as sometimes he will set a situation up to cause two people to become enemies. Some have referred to him as the "make-up sex" demon as it is his way of doing things.

W

Wadac: (Christian Demonology) Commonly known as the "Vice Demon", his job is to not only temp humans but to also tempt the Gods into giving in to vice. He has even been credited with the Birth of Jesus. As the transfer of abilities and power is done, when Jehovah took reign over the Main pantheon, he gained his succession from Zeus, who of course was always involved in adultery in some fashion. Jehovah though he tried at first could not shake these emotions that he had, and Wadac who was still a demi-god being turned into an angel for Jehovah's Army over heard some of Jehovah's complaints over the subject. Wadac, brought forth hundreds of human women, and had them throwing themselves at Jehovah, who in turn rejected the notion that he would give in to seduction on a human, as most gods refrained from this. Wadac then tried one last time, this time with three women. One of which was Mary, whom Jehovah gave in and seduced, thus he planted his seed in her, and she remained virgin. Jehovah who was distraught with his ease at giving in to a vice in this matter, lust cast Wadac in to Hell for 1,000 years, until Satan of course being a pain to Jehovah released him to let him cause vice to be the destruction of Man.

Ware:(Slavic Demonology) Was the half human daughter of Sonnilion, she was raped and murdered by Muslim Turks who invaded Romania in 1402. After she went through Purgatory before going to hell, she was granted the ability to return to Earth, where she is well known as a tormentor of Muslims and all followers of Allah.

Weland:(Mixed Demonology) Also known as Wieland, Wayland, and Volundr. This demon can be pretty much one of the most important demons known as you has heard of his doings, you just do not realize it. He once served in many pantheons mainly as the "blacksmith" and for much time deemed "good", but as time went on and the pantheons switched, he believed that Humans should know the intricate art of metal making and glass producing, so one day thousands of years ago he began that task, causing much outrage amongst the gods as he gave humans the two things that could both lead to the Gods demise, and even mankind's demise. However there was a real trick when he facilitated the use of the secret society known as the Masons. Now I must divulge this, even if you are a Mason, it does not mean that you are "worshipping the devil" nor are you "evil" it merely means that much like a lot of religions that have surfaced from time to time, even Christianity, that you are not researching your "religion of choice" to the fullest extent.

Wele Gumali:

(Mixed Demonology) Once a god in Kenya, early Witchcraft and Voodoo slaves worshipped him as a way to be "set free", and many slaves who called upon Wele Gumali successfully actually were free because their "slave owners" came to an untimely demise. It should be noted that recent rashes of worship to Wele Gumali have surfaced again, as recently as the Election of Barrack Obama to the President's Office. Though the cults that have been interviewed do claim a peaceful worship, there was one cult associated with the "Black Panthers" that was not as they practiced small animal sacrifices. This does follow the pattern found by a cult in 1977 in which there was one known human sacrifice; however the modern cults have not followed this route that we know of. But in all cases the sacrifice must be the second born child, of "white" in origins, preferably male.

X

Xamm:(Mixed Demonology) was once the portals keeper for the cross-worlds, has long since "retired" and is often seen near those areas where the portals are located on the planet, though does apparently have a constant sightings in Palm Bay, Florida which of course is the local portal for the region is just over by Lake Washington so I think it is a matter of a "working retirement" as his replacement for the job, She is very well known as to a liking for extended vacations. When she assumes human form, she normally appears as a well fit looking blond, however her eyes are peculiarly odd looking as her face takes on that of an animal in respect that the face is more on the side, and the eyes though human in form, happen to look as an animal does by being on both sides of the head.

Xa-Mul:(Asian Demonology) Known for his outrageous color, he usually appears in what can only be described as a "hunters orange" Gargoyle type appearance. He is known to act almost "gremlin" in behavior and is very well known to swallow a human whole. This is an ironic as, a minimum of 900,000 people go missing every year. And an interesting twist, there are reports of sightings in late July of 1975 by the Detroit area no less (and one of their worst summers in the past 100 years for missing persons reports.) He has recently as of 2009, has been seen in Central Africa.

Xaphan:(Christian Demonology) This former angel, though fallen is the chief fire demon in hell. Known to work the furnaces in central hell, he is described as a very skinny taller male when he takes human form, and very rarely is ever far away from the equator while here on earth. It should be noted that he is even seen wearing heavy winters clothing even if it is 90+ degrees (Fahrenheit)

Xastur:(Mixed Demonology) This demon is well known as a master of electricity through humans near death experience, easy way to tell if he is at work is to know someone or be someone who has had a severe near death experience, and Xastur is able to throw that persons spiritual center off balance and cause them to disable electrical devices, one of the most common devices are items such as wrist watches, light bulbs and magnetic devices.

Xatc:(Christian Demonology) This demon has become something of an oddity in the field of demonology, not only is she new, but she has a wicked taste for destruction, but yet in a few reports she has shown very peaceful attitudes toward humans. She normally takes the appearance of a human woman in her mid 20s, and in most cases the reports have shown she will wear glasses (almost horn-rimmed, or "cat's-eyes", popular in the retro Rockabilly/College social circles) and generally has darker hair, usually cut in what can be described as the "Bettie Page" style. The latest Report took place in Dayton, Ohio in which a Fraternity was taking pleasure in having some "special time" with an intoxicated and inebriated young female, whereupon Xatc (pronounced E-zat-ck) showed up and broke up the "party" Only two of the young men came forward as they have left the Fraternity and wished to keep their identities safe. They said "she came in and they all felt and got sick, vomiting everywhere. Then she smiled at them, and they all sodomized each other, and the entire time they could not scream, nor could they stop, after they were finished (which one states led to more vomiting) the girl "awoke" but was not really awake, almost zombie like and followed Xatc out of the frat house" The boys were rather scared when they were in the interview, and it should be noted that I am sure not all Fraternities take place in what can be considered "date-rape" or "drunk-rape". There are further reports from across the country and even Canada and the UK in which she has shown up and someone doing something which is considered morally wrong is smitten with a self induced punishment.

Xava (Kabbalah Demonology) Known as the demon that once stabbed Jehovah during the early Holy Wars, and is even said to be one of the cohorts who lead Lucifer to lash out against Jehovah, Xava is known to come to Earth to cause man pain, he will do everything from basics possession, to causing a family member to go insane and murder others. He is one of the best examples of what a demon is when people think of demon, we know he was here in 1949, as he was the demon that was cast out of a young 14 year old boy, which later became the inspiration for the novel and film, The Exorcist.

Xax: (Mixed Demonology) Known as the demon that has a special talent for destroying food, some feel as if she herself feeds off of hunger in humans and in animals. She is known to frequent restaurants and in most when the chef "just cannot get the order right" for yourself and others, she might be at play. She normally appears as a human female, medium brown hair, very striking hazel eyes, and commonly smells like what can only be described as sewage. She is polite to most humans who interact with her; however she hates chefs in any form as they make it impossible for her to feed.

Xerf: (Mixed Demonology) A succubus, known for her talent at tempting human males and females into riving in pleasure which is the energy to that she feeds from. She has been known to cause humans to be sexually attracted to her in her true form no less, which is interesting as most have described her as covered in a blue/green reptilian type skin, bright orange hair and eyes that would cause more of a fright in their reptilian version rather than an appealing human form. She is known to take human form generally with that of a "ginger" or "redhead" which does conform to the normal view of demonic shape shifting in which traits from demonic form are usually carried over to their human form. She is known to be a "self motivated" demon, however she will do favors for those whom ask, in some cases she has been known to disrupt marriages and relationships, but is known to keep away from situations in which she would be discovered as she dislikes scandals.

Xezbeth: (Mixed Demonology) One of the most powerful demons as she is the true demon of lies as she has been known to Lie to the God

Jehovah and even makes him believe the lies. She is ruled by Scorpios and can actually be commanded to serve them. However there is the downfall that whomever she serves, she will enable the ability to tell the strongest lies and cause them to be believed by others, but she will cause lies to grow larger then they can be even remotely controlled. In other words you can sit and eat lunch with someone and eat a salad, and with her power later tell the person that you ate a sandwich, however even something as trivial will be erupted and cause the lie to grow beyond control such as "you ate a sandwich made exclusively for you by a famous chef, to whom you are on a first name basis"

Xiang Yao: (Asian Demonology) Mainly a Chinese demon, though known to be throughout the Orient, this snake-like demon who is responsible for the great floods, who is the eternal opponent of the highest ruler for man. He is feisty if you let him into your home, however it is known that by deploying a mixture of garlic, salt, and ginger ground together into a paste, then deployed into the corners of your property will cause him to leave.

Xic: (Mixed demonology) If there was ever a record as to the sexuality of a demon, this one would fall into the "hates men with a passion Lesbian" She is known to lure men periodically to their death. Now it is not known if she feeds off of the male's demise, however some records have shown that when she first began her creation, she was in human form and living in Norway. She was apparently raped repeatedly by an invading clan, and since that time has been on a vengeance destroying and killing what men she can, however it is known she does target men who abuse women, especially those who at one time were considered Mafia. Some have suggested the Character of Anya in Buffy the Vampire Slayer was based off of Xic, however this cannot be confirmed. What can be confirmed is that she is one of the very first "vengeance demons" recorded, and she is known to seduce human women into lurid affairs over the centuries. She swears no loyalty to Satan, however in the same breath she swears no loyalty to Jehovah nor his son. She is known to visit pantheons where women (Goddesses) are in charge, and some have speculated she herself may be considered a god who looks over small "tribes" of women who band together in an Amazonia way.

Y

Yakshaia: (Hindu Demonology) Yakshaia is a chthonic semi-divine being, half god and half demon. He lives under the earth in the Himalayas where they guard the wealth of the earth, he has his workers find for his consumption items such as gems, gold, silver and zinc. However it is said Diamonds will destroy him. He is the brother of Kubera, the god of wealth.

Yalocan Tumulu: (Asian Demonology) Once known as the "Goddess of Fear" She came to become demon after Jehovah claimed the main pantheon as his own. She took sides with Lucifer when he began his fight for the throne, and some know that her abilities were strong enough to strike over 40 angels with fear (Which enabled Lucifer to claim the Eastern ridge over the Quantum

Mountains in the Heaven Pantheon, for almost 4 months.)

Yama:(Mixed Demonology) Though based in Asian Religions as the "King of Hell", he was reset once the pantheons were reset to reflect the energies built up by the west, Yama assumed his role as the king of the 5th dimensional pantheon of hell. He observes and rules over the Rapist of Religious Offenders as there has been a long tradition that regardless of how much a human can pray for forgiveness, the human is still considered a full sinner beyond redemption if they commit the act of rape and or turn their back on Jehovah, his son or what most religious scholars consider to be the "Trinity" No as those who wish to concede to the concept that Jesus died for yours and everyone's sins, that is not under debate. As mentioned in Luke 12:10, "Everyone who speaks against the Son of Man will be forgiven, but anyone who blasphemes against the Holy Spirit will not be forgiven" and again in Mark 3:29, "whoever blasphemes against the Holy Spirit can never be forgiven, as that person is holding the Eternal Sin" What all of this boils down to is this, if you have ever had doubt in the Holy Spirit, that would cover the Deity/god Jehovah in any form albeit any part of the "Trinity" then you have committed Eternal sin, which cannot be washed off by the Sacrificial Death of Jehovah's, son, Jesus. And on the side not of this subject, even though it is contained in the Book of Thomas, written around 46AD (or CE), the book is known to be a sourcebook of Thomas, a follower of Jesus, However they were not discovered until 1945 in Nag Hammadi, Egypt and is said to quote Jesus directly in Thomas 4:49 that "any man who takes pleasure with laying down with a woman against her will, shall know the Eternal sin, as a woman's pain will follow through life, so the mans will follow through Eternity" So regardless of how many times a prayer for forgiveness is proclaimed, if you have raped another person, thus their pain will last through their life, so shall yours as well, because any Eternal Sin cannot and will not be forgiven. Yama, will be your lord, and the rumors are is that he is fair, do your work, and you are eventually permitted to rest, however do not follow his orders and he is known to cast you in to a pit of hungry dogs for centuries on end.

Yaotzin: (Aztec Demonology) Formerly the Aztec God of "Hell" or at the very least their version of it, since the rise of Jehovah he has become a servant overlord demon for Satan in modern Hell. He has a knack for keeping the servants in line and has even been noted as the overlord in charge of taking in the new servants and making them available for any and all in the ranks of hell. Apparently he is efficient in his duties that he actually has been known to lead the servants for their services in Heaven as well and has been known to take regular vacations on Earth. He is fond of most cities on the planet that have a larger than average "gay" or homosexual population as he is known to take human form in what has only been described as a "Leather-boy" or "Biker Bear" and loves to be dominated when doing so. He is loyal to the humans he meets in his travels and is known to be kind and generous, to the point of being able to strike down anyone who upsets the human and making him a servant in Hell (Yes this has been confirmed by an American Evangelical Pastor who apparently condoned "fag-bashing" and Yaotzin was able to have him sent to hell upon death to be a servant.) It is said even Jehovah himself admires his dedication to service.

Yauhahu: (Mixed demonology) A demon that thrives on diseases and when they interact with humans, known also to love when humans are exposed to a new form of bacteria and virus that which they have not been exposed to yet, She is also known to be well active in Europe during the Plague eras. She is described as an "Old Hag" of a woman, who is known for her pasty pale skin, and even has the ability to adapt to different ethnic cultures to appear more solid with those she is haunting. She can emulate any known race of humans, and in each case she is described as an "older, haggy" looking lady with graying hair and eyes that are bright, white blue. She is known to also be a lover of the African Continent, and has been seen by people who come down with fevers and illness.

Yax: (Christian Demonology) Known as an assassin demon who has a taste for the soul of a human, however not just those who have tried to forfeit on a deal that they may have made with the devil, but will also go after the humans family and cause pain (Of course some would suggest the death of a loved one would be pain enough.) Yax has been known to claim the life once of a housewife in Michigan who made a deal to look no older than 25 until her death which was supposed to be 60, then she was to commit suicide, however she did not follow through, so Yax was the assassin demon sent, and she was killed, her 1st daughter was disabled, her second was somehow ended up in Detroit where she was repeatedly raped by a gang of thugs, and her son was injured in the very home where the woman had lived when a fire destroyed it, and her husband was killed by a following heart attack.

Yen-lo-Wang: (Asian Demonology) Once a ruler of Hell in Asian Pantheons, he later became the "Patron Saint of Child Molesters, Rapist and Thieves". Known to cause even a mother to consider her young child(ren) in a "not so tender and loving way", he is known to be attracted to any child or adult who appears to be blissfully happy and constantly (never stopping) going the extra measure to see that "eternal happiness, then have the flame of joy drenched in the water of tears from pain and suffering." Some religious historians and Demonologist have considered him to be the "Biggest Bastard" of the former Gods turned Demons. He does not swear allegiance under any flag other than his own, and is even known to have a human man try to "talk" to Jesus when he was 11, about "coming over to his house to see carvings", where as the intentions of Jesus' visit would be not as pleasant, so Jesus was intervened by Jehovah to not attend.

Yog-Sothoth: (Kabbalah Demonology) He is the Head Judge of Hell. Many know of the concept of the "Pearly Gates and St. Peter" and how that operates, well once you have been cleared into Hell, there is of course a central system that operates in very much the same way, some who have tried to escape Hell are brought before Yog. When he sits and judges you, he is known to put out even harsher torments on those who are "Damned" that Satan, Hades and the others before them. He likes the most cruel sentences, and according to a report that was passed along was said to sentence Muslims who have sinned to lick the genitals of Jewish sinners, and vice-versa. Christians, he enjoys making use of Anal based rape, as here when someone is raped it is no longer covered by "Eternal Sin" and is considered a fare punishment especially for those who lied to the public, knowingly, which I might point out is a blessing to know considering how many politicians there are in the world.)

DEMONOLOGY 101

Z

Zaebos: (Egyptian Demonology) Like a typical Egyptian God or Demi-God he is part human and is able to take on the appearance and characteristics of an animal, in his case that is a crocodile. Once the Egyptian Gods surrendered their control of the main pantheon, Zaebos spent some time working for Hades, and later Satan. He is known to have been upset with the Jesus/sacrifice situation as the followers whom he considered fanatics that should "be hung till they no longer pollute the Earth with their narrow-minded views" and feels and has stated that "no one religion should dominate man in such a vile way to the point of not having a free will" and has been known to even been blessed by Jehovah (Jesus' father) with the ability to do as he pleases to whomever he pleases on the planet as even Jehovah adores the concept of "free will" and Zaebos is known to cause most humans to "tempt sin" in small doses as a way to live their lives and be happy, one of his favorite is letting humans give in to sexual desires, as he much like a lot of the previous gods only feel heterosexual sex is a way of making the human race (and others) grow and create strong numbers.

Zagam:

(Kabbalah Demonology) This demon is special in respect that his known spells are the talent of deceit and falsehoods. He knows how to falsify objects and even people and other gods, angels and demons. He is able to do his spells so well; that even Jehovah had Zagam teach Jesus the abilities during his "hidden time" so Jesus was able to perform the "miracle" of turning water into wine. (One must remember, that even though one is given the abilities of being a god, you do not automatically know how to perform tasks and must seek tutoring, and given light that Zagam is a demon, he is not under the care of Satan, and is even known to be able to cross over into the Heaven Pantheon at will. So the use of Jehovah to teach his son the use of an ability is not that un-heard of, as the former god Poseidon was the teacher to Jesus as to navigate the walking on water.)

Zagan:

(Christian Demonology) Known as the leader of 33 legions, he is also known as a Grand King in the western region of Hell. He is known to be a fair demon; however he does swear full allegiance to Satan. He is known to come to Earth every so often and the most recent was during the initial conflict in the Middle East. He is described in human form as having a grayish hue to his skin, with what most say is red-bloodshot eyes. He is known that during the last 3 Holy Wars to be an honorary General and has a passion for military fighting.

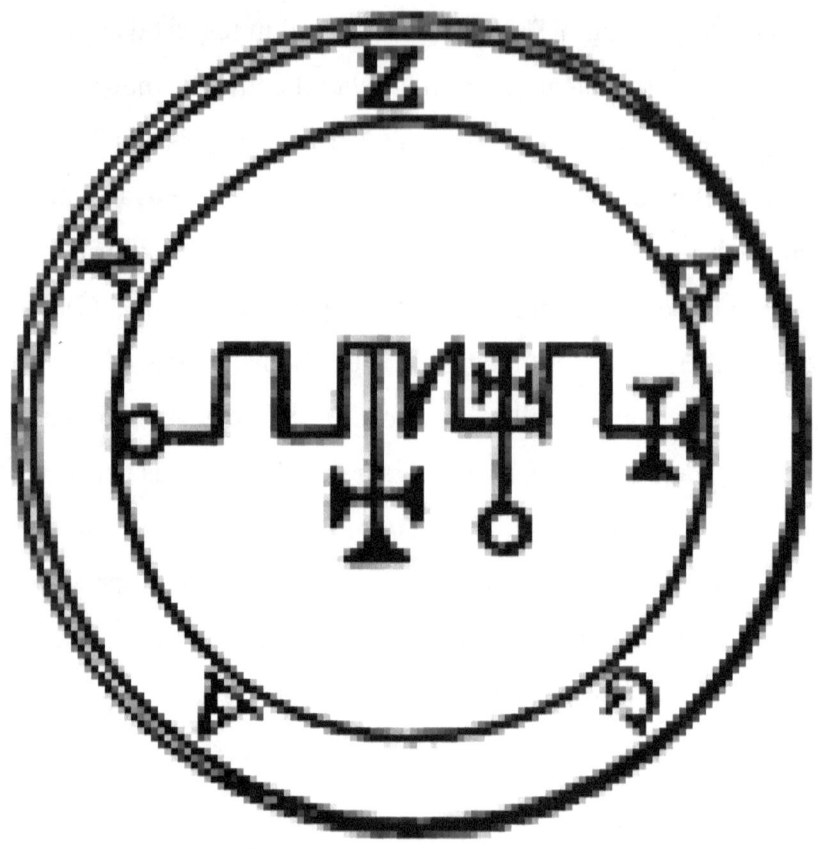

Zabulon:(Kabbalah Demonology) She is a demon, who possesses one of the seals of Omega, which if gathered with the other 4 seals would end life on the planet. We know that one seal was in possession of Gabriel, who of course disposed of it to an unknown source, and that the other two seals are now in the care of Earth. Though no humans have claimed to posses the seals, we know they are still retained in safe locations. (One in the Vatican, the other is in the care of a well "booby-trapped" Babylonian Temple.) She is to some degree a good demon as she possesses the seal and will fight to keep possession as she does not feel mankind should have access to its power let alone the capability to destroy mankind's future. She is known to have black hair and dark eyes when she takes human form.

Zapan: (Kabbalah Demonology) Once was the very King of Hell, before the beginning of all the Holy Wars. He is known to now not care for any of it and even visits the positive pantheons to see his former enemies, now his friends. He is known to have even sat on the council before Lucifer caused havoc, and even is considered a friend to Jehovah. He reflects on his former glory of military battles and is even known to "possess" different human military leaders from time to time just to put out a battle plan and see if it works. (And he is known not really to take sides on said matters; it is just a way to see how it works out.)

Zapd: (Mixed Demonology) Though the origin of this demon is mixed, we know that his's/her's/it's (Sex unknown) origination comes from early Sumerian society. Zapd is well known by most demonologists who study the subject as the one who "cause relatives to take the life of a child" We know the demon thrives on the energy caused by a parent or a loved one who takes the life of their own child. The demon commonly appears as an African American Male, or as a Caucasian Woman, both with dark hair and light eyes. Now the demon does not commit the killing, however the demon can cause the brain to reconsider the situation in a "as a matter of fact" way such as making a parent seeing how "much better life would be without the child" or how "the child could be set free of suffering" The only way to defeat Zapd (Pronounced Zah-ped) is to pour a warm bath typical in size to cleanse the adult, and use mo less than 30 ounces of powdered milk (such as Cow's milk) wearing silver jewelry. Bath in the water for no less than one hour, proclaiming that love for the child, (Optional - and if decided the child's life will be safe under the care of a deity.) The child's life will be safe, as Zapd doesn't appear to pick a child to have killed for sake of the child, but as for what the older adult (and in three cases an older siblings) life destruction means to Zapd. Once Zapd has chosen you, it would be best to rid yourself of the attention.

Zaxas:

(Egyptian Demonology) The demon known for causing the rivers to rise when they shouldn't and more importantly known for pulling small children into the water. The second most recent report was from 2003 in El-Mahalla El-Kubra, Egypt. However in as recent as 2011, there was a report of Zaxas actually seen in Georgia, USA. This would account for the lack of appearances in the Egyptian homeland, and also reaffirm the accounts throughout history of Zaxas being spotted in areas away from Egypt. Zaxas is known to take almost a brown/dark red tone, and have 12 tentacles almost squid like in appearance, but it is not the average squid size. The report taken near the Lake Sidney Lainer as it crosses the Buford Dam over into the Chattahoochee River, and later by the Morgan Falls Reservoir. The body from tip of a tentacle to the top of the head is described at about 120 feet long. Unfortunately there was a known loss of life in the incident, as a dog, reported as a Boxer was seen taken by Zaxas, possibly for food.

Zayax:

(Mixed Demonology) Once known as the "Prince of the Water and Oceans", he now is a demon. When the last of the Holy Wars transpired, he felt Jehovah was ruthless and mean-spirited, so he took sides for Lucifer. He is known to posses the power of getting into any room, in any building anywhere as long as it is hooked up to a water supply. He is even known to be able to move through land water. He is known to take humans lives; however he has a "trickster" side in which he loves to torment humans with his acts. He was spotted in 1992 in Chicago, Illinois and as some have theorized as seeing him in the flood waters, even though it was blamed on a construction mishap, most demonologist believe he had something to do with it. He can assume any form, and has been known to take a human shape, however the sightings all agree, he is as clear as water.

Zeernebooch:

(Mixed Demonology) Though based in early Germanic/Celtic religions as the "King of the Dead" he wasn't considered evil until the rights of Jehovah and his climb to power on the main pantheon and he refused to consider Jehovah as a leader. Even Satan is fearful of him as it is said that upon Zeernbooch's will the dead will walk the Earth, thus causing the "End of Days" for humans. He had done it once in the year 1146 in southern Europe in which 3 entire villages were destroyed as Zeernebooch figured he would unleash the dead upon man, to which even Jehovah and Satan themselves argued against it and negotiated with him. Under the plans of the Negotiation, Only when Jehovah and Satan are in compliance with each other would the dead be unleashed by Zeernbooch, however Zeernbooch being Zeernbooch left 4 seals on the earth, if they are all gathered in the same location and activated by the spell provided upon them, the will of Zeernbooch would be unleashed, and the dead will rise. It is known that the possessor of a seal would have the capability of raising one dead person per passing of the moon, and that the person would in effect be brought back with no "zombie-like" side effects.

Zephar:

(Christian Demonology) Also known as Zepar, he is a special demon; the powers that have been recorded with Zephar are countless. He is known to drive women insane and not in a good way. He has a talent for having children disturbed by making adult males and females take advantage of children sexually. He was once considered a "God of war" and is well known for his tactics of encasing the enemy by fire on all sides. Under the last few Holy Wars, he has ascended to the rank of a Grand Duke, he is known to command 26 legions, and is well known to have taken the eternal lives of angels. *(See seal symbol on next page)*

Seal of Zephar, aka Zepar

Zlothos:

(Mixed demonology) Was once a human, and is well known for her charms against other women. She has been spotted recently as if 2011 in Georgia, USA. She is known to not really have allegiance for Satan, more for her own selfish power struggle. Some have even stated that among the demons, if you are able to help her gain power, she will be very loyal to you. She normally appears with dark auburn hair and green eyes. Described as very attractive, apparently feeds upon the thoughts of others who find her attractive. She is known to take humans lives if they stand in her way, however as stated she has no allegiance to Satan, so it has come to no surprise that she has been known to even attend churches on Sundays.

Zimimar:

(Mixed Demonology) If there was ever a demon who deserved the gratitude of the United States Government's Counter Intelligence, it would be this very demon. He is that demon who basically writes and conceives any and all propaganda pertaining to Hell, Satan, The Dark Forces. He is known to be able to facilitate himself into humans, possessing them and is even reported to be the one who came up with the "grape Kool-Aid" concept for Jim Jones. He is known to take form around humans as well, and has been seen conversing with political advisor, Karl Rove and Social Advertiser Richard Berman. Zimimar is the master of twisting and spinning a subject to make it sound almost appealing to anyone. In human form, he mainly takes on a white/Caucasian tone, balding and always likes to eat.

Known Demonic Races

Outside of the known individual demons, there are known races of demonic types of spirits. Some are prone to air, or water and even land. It depends really on a lot of who was in charge of the main pantheons when they were formed and sometimes even on what dimensional realm they hail from.

Ahremanes:

These were former Angels, who "Fell from Grace" during the Holy Wars, or even during a non-war period in which they acted against the ruler of the main Heaven Pantheon. Their name actually was given to them by the Persians, during the Persians early religion period (which some call the forerunner to Judaism, which of course gives roots to Christianity in its first form of Catholic, and eventually the Protestant version (Remember Evangelical is only as old as the 1950s) These demons resemble the basic personification of what people deem as a "demon" and in most cases what people think if when they think of the Devil, himself. They can have a difference in skin color, such as dark reds, greens, blues, and a dark grey/black. However they generally have wings, which appear bat-like.

Alfar:

These demons are known for their relationship to the Nordic Gods. They are the opposite of the "trolls" however known to resemble trolls as well. When they cross dimensional realms, they like to cause diseases and nightmares in humans, Gods and even known to "haunt" other demons.

Alrunes:

There have been well known stories of the Alrunes, they are commonly referred to as "Amazons" by humans. They can take different shapes and races of humans, and animals, however they never change their race. They are known to torture human males, and will take "gathering trips" to Earth in order to gather more "breeding stock." It is known that if they do give birth to a son, the son is considered faulty and sacrificed. They live for what can be considered 11 millennium (11,000 years +) so they only take breeding stock of human males rarely.

Amon:

This race is known for living in typical Demonic Tribal settings. They only interact with humans and others at their accord. If you are caught in their realm, it is known that those people rarely make it out alive. When they do interact, it is known they like to resemble the Egyptian Gods, and will take human form with animal traits and body parts.

Bayemonites:

This tribe of demons, which is nothing more than an offshoot of the Daevas Race, formed their own tribe during the 11th century. They are peaceful demons for the better degree, however it is known that their tribe is very much enabling humans with occult magick. They write grimoires and leave them in places aimed at making sure humans find them. In some cases they will leave a partial grimoire of their more powerful spells in one spot, and will leave the other half in another place to cause the "human to drive for what they wish". They are also capable of very powerful talisman engineering; in fact most who have used their talismans find it is some of the most powerful in their possession.

Cacodaemons:

These demons have some of the lesser magickal power compared to other known races, however they do have a strong enough will to endure whatever they need to accomplish their task. They worship Hades, and when the holy war broke out in which Hades "handed over Hell, to Jehovah, for Jehovah's choice as to who should run the Underworld" the Cacodaemons showed their loyalty by ignoring Jehovah's Choice of Satan and even known to helping out Jewish Rabbis and Christian's in their fight against Satan. Most humans fear them as their appearance is generally a larger than human stature and a blackish hue to their skin, and even though they will help anyone who is against Satan, they are still regarded as Evil due to appearance.

Cambions:
When Incubus and Succubus mate their offspring are Cambions. However much like that mating of a Mule and a Horse, the offspring doesn't have the capability to reproduce, and more importantly where sexual energy is absorbed by its parents, any and all sexual energy will actually harm and even lead to death. Cambions generally have a lifespan of about 700 human years, and have actually been known to be accepted by Jehovah and most Cambions who live on Earth will actually attend churches. They are easy to spot as they never really take on a mate.

Catabolignes:

Known as a race of warrior demons, they constantly did battle and to some degree have been reduced to a tribe of mercenaries. They can be conjured for hiring, however make sure you have plenty of wheat or gold. They will work for nothing less.

Chevaliers:

These demons are regarded as "workers" by the deities and humans who conjure them. They can be killed by apples, albeit thrown at them or even sprayed by apple sauce. They can only be conjured at sunrise or at sunset and will go back to their dimensional realm the following day change.

Ciupipiltin:

These demons are what most people recognize as a "Vampire" from traditional lore. They will not go in sunlight, and fest on blood or the "life-force" commonly found in blood. There have been human hybrids caused by breeding, thus the hybrid does take on more of the human form, however they are very well known for keeping their tribes secret as much as possible from man.

Daevas:

This class of demon is very attracted to the unclean. If there is a prostitute human, she would attract these demons as the prostitute would be considered "unclean", when most Daevas come to earth they are known for playing in brothers and being "street-edge" or "streetwise" as far as where they would be found. They are disgusted with soaps and most "flowery fragrances". However it should be pointed out that they are very, very loyal. If you are asked for a hand out from one, and you give them some money, even a small amount you will have a "protector" that would even severely beat someone if they threaten you or your known property (when I say "known property" such as they see you leave your car parked on the street, and incidentally I would like to report that not only is this report true, but all I can say is "my vehicle, parked in the worst area of Atlanta, Georgia and the best seventy-five cents I ever gave to someone.) the Daevas will try to hide their demonic form when asking for money, however I have it on good knowledge that when you please them by giving them money, their eyes go a bit serpent like yellow.

Daityas:
They are a race of Demons who are very large. The average heights of them are about 15 feet high. They normally live by the seashores, and not on land, but generally in the 12-20 mile region located by the seashore underwater. They can make time on land; however they are usually against people of the land. They have no problem with humans providing they do not invade their villages under the waves, and will even accept visitors, providing the visitor does not disturb

their life such as youngling hatcheries and so forth. It is said they do however get angry when man contaminates the ocean and are also known to have a temper on the subject as well. There are a few more ship incidents involving unexplained accidents with the Oil companies that they would like to admit, let alone report. They are an offshoot tribe of the Fomors Tribes of Demons.

Diriel:

These demons were not known as of late as the 19th century, however more light has come on them, they are commonly known as "thought demons" by humans, they have the ability to strike fear into humans by sight alone, and when they are present they can strike fear into most humans to cause them to flee the area. We know of four settlements of the Diriel living on the planet. Three of which are found in America, Mid-State West Virginia actually harbors their biggest village, also found in southern Georgia and Northern Michigan. There is also a known settlement in Southeastern Romania, just outside the City of Tecuci.

Empusae:

They are a race of demons who were once all humans. They followed the Hecate cults in between the 4th and 8th centuries. Even though being involved with Witchcraft and or Satanic Magick are not actual paths to Hell, the Empusae were direct followers of Hecate and more importantly they gave their souls to her. Though on occasion she does actually collect a few souls here and there, she is known to have a bond to a person once they give their soul, thus once the human asks for forgiveness to Jehovah and or his son, sure the person can be forgiven, however Hecate does not forgive, nor does she allow any being to own the souls in which she possesses. When you are turned from the living world to the afterlife, your soul if promised to Hecate, you will be "re-born" as her children.

Fomors:
These ancient tribes of Celtic subaquatic demons have been described in detail in books dating as far back as the 11th century. Their exploits and lifestyles have been described and passed down to demonologist over the centuries. They commonly live in the underwater island of Lochlan and are known for terrorizing the coastline of County Donegal with what has been described as "Seeing the Titanic herself, underwater and thrashing about". They are large and in their environment they are in charge. They look often for food and as recent as 2011 there have been reports of missing boats.

Galla:

This tribe of demons is better known for the seven demons called Galla. They hail from the Sumerian underworld and are known to on occasion roam the planet Earth and hunt for men, women, and children to haul back to that pantheon, and will torture and dine on the humans until they are dead and eaten, then they will resume the looking. In some cases entire human families will disappear. The only way to fight them off is by throwing salt or cheese (especially blue cheese) in their direction. The salt and or cheese is known to burn them, and they will leave in an attempt to garner another target. In 1944 the US Government made an attempt to capture one, however the Galla were aware and in turn gained over a hundred men that day for food, to which they were not seen again until 1993. They have been here again in 1997, 2001, 2003, 2007 and the very last was in January 2011.

Ghul:

Pronounced the same as Ghoul, these are female demons that can assume the shape of an animal. They are known in almost every desert, and some refer to them as the demonic race equal to Sirens in the seas. They are known for taking more of as human form and finding men or women in populated areas, a tribe of them were exterminated by Las Vegas, Nevada in 2009, however some have still reported sightings in the Mojave desert as of August, 2011.

Goblins:
This race of demons is closely related to Fearies or "the Fae", however much as the name suggest, they are not the "cute" type. Goblins are common around winter and summer seasons as they enjoy the extreme temperatures, also it should be noted that humans commonly call them Gremlins.

Gorgons:
Though most who understand Greek Religion/Mythology like to attribute the Gorgon race to their belief system, it is in fact a race of demonic soldiers who despite their base in being a demon, they usually take on human traits as they live out their lives amongst humans no less. They will take up residence amongst other humans, be polite and courteous to their neighbors, however they really do not go into any deep conversations with their neighbors outside of the average "how about the weather" so to speak. They usually keep to their selves, and are known to invite in "relatives" for gatherings. However the relatives are either true relatives or other gorgons. They like to usually have a party which most people associate with Halloween, as called the "Feast of Medusa" generally held around the first Saturday of November. One thing they do like to be present is mushroom dishes, however it is now known that the years of interbreeding humans and Gorgons have led to odd reactions and

allergies to certain things. One of the most notable allergies these hybrid Human/Gorgon races have is the allergies to tree nuts. This would stem from the initial crossbreeding of Gorgons and Jewish Humans in the late 4th Century BC, when a few villages in Israel harbored refugees left over from the Gorgon conflict that took place between Jehovah and some of the earlier pantheons.

Guecubu:

These demons are known to haunt the woodlands and jungles on the South American continent. They for the better degree are considered evil because they do like to terrorize villages and communities.

Hiisi:

This race of demons loves to inhabit the colder regions of the planet. Though there is a village of them that happens to exist in Canada just north of Willmore Wilderness Park, which apparently actually enjoys a brief period of summer. In any case the Hiisi (pronounce Hee-See) are actually quite nice, however because mankind has wondered into their village, they do and will kill a human on site in fear of being discovered by man. Centuries ago they would lay waste to entire Finnish Villages that were "too close for comfort" to their own villages.

Incubus:

They are this race of demons is actually loaners. They are known to be a male demon, and more known for their sexual escapades as advertised against women, however most overlook that they still consummate sex with male humans as well (as much as the female Succubus does with human females as well) They have been known to be attracted to anyone of "weak stature" albeit it male or female, and when the human least suspects it, they will attack. They will give signs of their presence in order to gain larger amounts of fear (most think Incubi or Succubi feast on sexual energy, however this has proven half true. In the Proctor Case in 1987, the family that was attacked was providing great fear against the Incubus attacking, and this in lead led to the discovery that it was the fear that was keeping the Incubus around the family's home.) In some cases of attack there has even been the presence of bodily fluid left as evidence, which is ironic as when the DNA is tested there is no known type and the person who has suffered the attack will call the police, and at the attending hospital a "rape kit" or a sexual attack evidence gathering kit will be dispensed, they gather the DNA and in two known cases (One male victim and one female) have charged them with raping an animal in a bestiality charge, which is generally dismissed as the "Animal" is never identified.

Jinn:

These demons are commonly known through other names, the most popular is the name of Genie, and no it does not mean that some skimpy blond gal is going to be calling you master if you happen to summon one, people often think of Satan offering wishes to humans and each wish having a negative effect, which is how the Jinn got such a bad reputation, because humans associate creatures with one another based upon positive or negative aspects. However the negative effect is in fact because humans try to complicate the wish. They ask to win the lottery and never say jackpot, so they win the lottery and usually gain their betting money back. Or people say things like "make me famous" and then they end up being on the receiving end of death by a serial killer. The Jinn in fact just like freedom. Also, it should be noted, most people assume three wishes, which is not the truth however. Some Jinn can do hundreds and even lifetimes amounts of wishes; it depends on the slavery spell which was cast upon them by Allah.

Mandragoras:

These demons are easily conjured with the use of Mandrake root. However in order to banish them one needs to make sure they use Mandrake root again and a mixture of Vinegar and salt in the banishment spell. It is known that they will appear almost "hobbit" like, with beards and will serve the conjurers wish, however they are true demons in the Christian sense in that they are true followers of

Satan. They thrive on rebellion and it does cause them to bring out their best work in their task if the person who conjured them is intent on truly hurting or destroying a target. They are known to have a good resistance to Holy Water if the water is not impregnated with Vinegar and Mandrake root (Holy Water commonly has some salt in it as when the Church barrowed the recipe for positive waters made from the early Pagan religions)

Nagas:

These demons like to form that of a larger serpent, they are known to frequent lakes and river and are known to can be called upon to lash out at an enemy. The only way to rid yourself of them is by covering yourself in flour, and even to the point of dumping a good amount of flour into the body of water where they frequent.

Pretas:

These demons are prone to attacking humans by re-animating a dead body with their energy and even going to the extent of re-animating animals. They can be vanquished from attacking you by decapitating the corpse. They are known to have ties to the Hindu faith, however were once involved in Egypt, ironically during the time the concept of "The Mummy coming back" myth. It is known that owning a cat will cause them to not be attracted to your home, and they are known to like water.

Seiktha:

These demons prefer the forest land, and are known to attack humans if they venture into their local. There are villages known in Washington State, Rendlesham Forest in the UK and in a few Tennessee and Kentucky forest (Daniel Boone state forest no less)

Succubus:

These are the female equals of the Incubus type of demons. They are known for their sexual escapades and feasting on sexual energy. However it is known they feast on fear as well. It should be noted that there have been cases in which the Succubus has gained a half human, half demon child from the union. Some of the offspring have been living in the Hell regions, while even a few even live in the other pantheons, and most notably Earth. However the children that are produced that live on Earth are forbidden by rights of the current Holy Treaty to serve as a politician, medical doctor and law enforcement. To this it can be noted that they are permitted, though this may sound as a bad joke, as a lawyer. The only reason why I consider it a bad joke as I happen to know of two who are lawyers.

Tase:

If there was ever a race of demons that could pass themselves off as Vampires it would have to be the Tase who could easily be considered the most acceptable for the translation. They are demons of women scorned by being an unwed mother, and if they happen to die during childbirth, when they return as Tase, they will take on more Succubi traits, feeding off of the sexual and fear energies, however the male Tase which are born out of a variety of ways, are more prone to torturing women and children. They are known for wars against other houses and races of demons as they feel they should be in the prime light as those feared by humans. And can assume shape-shifting at ease, they can be defeated by the ususal garlic, salt and holy water. However an interesting bit is that gold will affect them very much like a human drunk, and silver doubly so. They rarely drink blood, however it is known that they will consider drinking a human's blood if he or she was hard to kill, which ironically lead to the Tase being infected by HIV.

Vodnik:

These demons are born from the drowning death of a child, they normally appear almost as a human, only with a scale like skin, and commonly have green hair in different shades. If the child is murdered by drowning the Vodnik has more power rather than those who were born from an accidental death, and even though their kind originated in Russia, they have been seen around the world. They are known to liquefy themselves and are able to travel along in pipes, also they can in their human type form walk on the planet, but require water. The most recent sightings of a Vodnik demon is actually two of them are known to live in South Carolina by Lake Murray and the local smaller lakes and reservoirs, and will eat most rodents, water creatures and in almost a dozen cases they have attacked pleasure boaters and those who are fishing, no human attacks thankfully, but there have been some dogs who were along to accompany their human companions who were lost however.

Yaksha:

These race of demons is known for their legacy as that of an almost Cthuonic semi-divine beings, they have been described as "Half-God and Half-Demon". They have had run ins with Jehovah and even Satan. They do not swear allegiance for either side in the current holy political system; however they are prone for occasionally disrupting the health and welfare of evangelical followers. The Yaksha love gold and gems, and are known to rob it from humans, as they feel it is theirs to begin with, because they often live below ground.

DEMONOLOGY 101

Bibliography and Suggested Reading

Bardon, F. (1962). *Initiation Into Hermetics.* Osiris-Verlag.
Baroja, Julio (1975). *The World of the Witches.* University of Chicago Press.

Barrett, Frances (1999). *The Magus Book 1 & 2: A Complete System of Occult Philosophy.* Book Tree (modern copy)

Barrett, F. (1801) *The Magus books 1,2,and 3.* Lackington Alley and CO. (It should be noted some information gathered was from side notes written by Barrett from his manuscripts as well)

Baker, Douglas. (1977) *Practical Techniques of Astral Projection,* Weiser,
Begley, Walter. (1903*) BIBLIA CABALISTICA.* London/D. Nutt

Black, Jeremy (1992). *Gods, Demons and Symbols of Ancient Mesopotamia.* University of Texas Press

Blofeld, J. (1968). *The Book of Change.* George Allen & Unwin.

Belanger, Michelle (2010). *The Dictionary of Demons: Names of the Damned.* Llewellyn Publications.
Brennan, J.H.(1971*).* *Astral Doorways.* Aquarian-Wellingborough,
Budge, E.A. Wallis(1895). *THE BOOK OF THE DEAD*: The Papyrus of Ani. British Museum.
Cavendish, R. (1975). *The Tarot.* Michael Joseph Pub.
Conway, David.(1974). *Magic; an Occult Primer.* Mayflower Press
Conway, David(1972). *Ritual Magic, An Occult Primer,* Dutton.

Crowley, Aleister (1977). *777 and other Qabalistic Writings of Aleister Crowley,* Weiser,

Crowley, Aleister (1995). *The Goetia: The Lesser Key of Solomon the King: Lemegeton - Clavicula Salomonis Regis.* Weiser Books

Davidson, Gustav (1994) *A Dictionary of Angels: Including the Fallen Angels.* Free Press

Denning, Melita and Phillips, Osborne(1979) *Llewellyn Practical Guide to Astral Projection, The,* Llewellyn.

Guiley, Rosemary (1999). *The Encyclopedia of Witches and Witchcraft.* Checkmark Books.

Hartmann, F.(1913) *Geomancy.* Rider Press)

Hyatt, Victoria (1974). *The Book of Demons.* Lorrimer Publishing Limited

Knight, G.(1965) *A Practical Guide To Qabalistic Symbolism (Vol 2).* Helios Press

Mack, Carol (1999). *A Field Guide to Demons, Fairies, Fallen Angels and Other Subversive Spirits.* Holt Paperbacks

Mathers, S.L. MacGregor(1972) Astral *Projection, Magic and Alchemy.* Neville Spearman.

Mathers, S.L.M.(*trans.*)(1914) *GreaterKey ofSolomon, The,* De Laurence, Scott & Co.

Meillissoux-Le Cerf, Micheline(1992) *Dom Pernety et les Illuminés d'Avignon* Milano-Arché.

Moser, R.E.(1974). *Mental and Astral Projection,* Esoteric Publications.

Ponce. C. (1932). *The Kabbalah. Garnstone,* London.

Regardie, I.(1933). *The Tree Of Life.* Rider Press

Regardie, I.(1937-40) *The Golden Dawn (4 Vols).* Aries Press.

Rémy, Nicholas (1974). *Demonolatry.* University Books.

Shah, I.(1972). *The Secret Lore of Magic.* Abacus.

Waite, A.E.(1960) *The Pictorial Key To The Tarot.* University Books.

Weed, Joseph(1973) *Wisdom of the Mystic Masters,* Reward Books.

Welz, K.H. (1992) *Talismanic Magick.* HST

Weyer, Johann (1991). *Witches, Devils, and Doctors in the Renaissance.* **Mrts-Pub.**

ABOUT THE AUTHOR

K.W.Kesler was born in Ohio, lives life much like you do, loves to go places and see and do many things. He has gained communication degrees, worked at places such as everything from fast food, to museums. He has been interested and studied the Occult for the better degree of his life, and is constantly still investigating incidents and occurrences of paranormal situations whenever they are presented to him.

www.ingramcontent.com/pod-product-compliance
Lightning Source LLC
Chambersburg PA
CBHW031600170426
43196CB00031B/251